MAN AND MEMORY

MAN AND MEMORY

D. S. HALACY, JR.

1817

HARPER & ROW, PUBLISHERS

NEW YORK AND EVANSTON

Grateful acknowledgment is made to the following for permission to use the previously published material as cited below.

From D. P. Kimble (ed.), *The Anatomy of Memory, Volume 1.* Palo Alto, California: Science and Behavior Books, 1965.

From *Stop Forgetting,* by Bruno Furst. Copyright 1948, 1949 by Bruno Furst. Reprinted by permission of Doubleday & Company, Inc.

From *Persistence Transfer,* by J. G. Nicholls et al.; *Science,* vol. 158, pp. 1524–1525, 22 December 1967. Copyright 1967 by the American Association for the Advancement of Science. By permission of the Association and the author.

From *Techniques for Effective Remembering,* by Eleanor C. Laird and Donald A. Laird. Copyright 1960 by Eleanor C. and Donald A. Laird. Used with permission of McGraw-Hill Book Company.

From *Memory,* by Walter de la Mare. Reprinted with the permission of The Society of Authors, London, as representatives of The Literary Trustees of Walter de la Mare.

From *The Cerebral Cortex of Man,* by Wilder Penfield and Theodore Rasmussen. Copyright 1950 by The Macmillan Company. Reprinted with permission of The Macmillan Company.

CONTENTS

MAN AND MEMORY

Chapter One

INTRODUCTION

An anonymous little girl spoke for most of us when she pronounced that "My memory is the thing I forget with." Memory also helps us worry. A poor memory and a clear conscience go together, and a poor memory helps a man to be satisfied with himself. Perhaps we joke about memory because we don't understand it. We don't understand gravity or electricity either, but we manage to put these forces to use and to live with them. Of all the phenomena we don't understand, memory ranks high on the list. Without memory there would be nothing: no books, no television, no money, no homes—no human beings. For it is the ability to recall the past that makes learning and communication possible.

Man did not understand the reproductive process until quite recently in his history, but he reproduced nevertheless. Now so much is being learned about biological processes that a biological revolution is taking place. Man seems to be not only zeroing in on the secrets of life in nature but also learning how to produce life artificially. Paralleling this development is a revolution in the field of memory.

A few years ago neurophysiologist W. Ross Ashby, formerly head of the famous Burden Neurological Institute in England and now at the University of Illinois, concluded a paper with this plea:

> Finally, I commend as a program for research, the *identification of the physical basis of the brain's memory stores*. Our knowl-

edge of the brain's functioning is today grossly out of balance. A vast amount is known about how the brain goes from state to state at about millisecond intervals; but when we consider our knowledge of the basis of the important long-term changes we find it to amount, practically, to nothing. I suggest it is time that we made some definite attempt to attack this problem. Surely it is time that the world had *one* team active in this direction?

Although Ashby was correct in his appraisal of the state of knowledge of the physical basis of memory, this dearth of knowledge was not due to neglect of the problem.

In 1969 a scientific journal pointed out that many molecular biologists are convinced that the "golden era" of the biological revolution has ended and are now turning their attention, as well as their techniques, to study of the brain. The study of memory has also become a fertile field for psychologists, physiologists, mathematicians, physicists, and scholars in many other disciplines.

It is understandable that neurological institutes and similar organizations should be searching diligently for the mechanism of memory; in addition, however, this search has received backing from many government agencies, including the military. Memory symposia are held annually; in 1968 the United Nations, in collaboration with its offspring, the International Brain Research Organization, held a conference on brain research and its application to human behavior.

Considering its scope, the revolution in memory research is a strangely quiet one. Perhaps part of the caution stems from wild misunderstandings that have greeted some research projects in the past. Press releases on a brain model called a *perceptron* resulted in a rash of "Navy builds monster brain" scare stories, and such publicity hardly bodes well for the success of a program of dignified scientific research. In what might be a self-conscious attempt to offset such bogeyman tales, the memory detectives publish such journals as the outrageously funny *Worm Runner's Digest,* which is filled with delicious satire, poems, and cartoons joshing the memory workers and their "beasts." Joining the fun, Arthur Koestler coined the expression "ratomorphism" to describe the thinking processes of psychologists who fill their black boxes with those animals.

A few years ago an eminent scientist called for a crash program to discover the remaining secrets of life. No such pleas have yet been made for memory research; however, the magnitude of the research effort is surprising. Many teams have worked on the identification of the physical basis of the brain's memory stores. Those who have been involved for many years in the search include Ramon y Cajal of Spain, Karl Lashley of the United States, and Donald Hebb and Wilder Penfield of Canada, to name a few. More recently the search has been joined by Holger Hydén of Sweden, Sir John Eccles of Australia, Peter Uttley of England, Warren McCulloch, John von Neumann, Fritz von Foerster, James McConnell, Georges Ungar, Roger Sperry, Frank Rosenblatt, and others.

Both research teams and individual scientists are increasing the attack on several fronts by probing the brain with microelectrodes, by dosing it with drugs, by excising pieces of it, and by studying it as a "black box"—or a "pink box" as it has been called in deference to its characteristic color. Elaborate models of the brain—or at least what researchers hope are crude facsimiles —have been constructed and put through their paces at learning. The computer, or so-called electronic brain, was hailed as being patterned after the brain and thus as being a model of the brain, but as yet this approach has not been too fruitful.

The scientists who study dreams are assisting in the search. Dreams stem from memory, as illustrated by the story of a young lady who dreamed that a knight on a white charger spirited her away to a secret bower and deposited her, breathless and petrified, under a tree. When she asked in a whisper what he was going to do next, the knight shrugged and said, "I don't know, lady. It's your dream."

Surprisingly, science took a long time to pin down the physical location of memory. Memory was once thought to be located in the stomach or the liver. Even in fairly recent times, scientists have located memory in the spine or even in the retina of the eye. Some early researchers ascribed to the pineal gland the property of mind and memory, and Sigmund Freud seemed to be trying to tie memory to the sex glands.

Part of the preparation for the search included the mechanics of measuring memory, and Hermann Ebbinghaus, a German, pioneered in this field. Other scientists tied memory to intelligence, and Sir Francis Galton designed the first intelligence tests. Binet and his followers have produced the more sophisticated IQ tests, all of which include memory as a prime factor. Scientists have made a rough count of neurons, or brain cells, and have discovered that they total over ten billion in a single human—a number three times the present population of the earth. Other men have succeeded in dissecting both neurons and tinier components and in weighing the increase in certain neuronal chemicals concomitant with the acquisition of memories.

Not surprisingly, little or no agreement exists as to the actual mechanism of memory. There have been and continue to be various theories to account for the storage and recall of perceptions. Is memory a fixed "circuit" in the brain, linking neurons together much like a circuit in a computer? Or is memory instead the pattern of electrical or other activity, perhaps shared by all parts of the brain rather than resident in a single location? Here is the dilemma: Lashley cut away great portions of brain with no apparent reduction in memory power; yet Penfield touched a certain area in the brain and stimulated memories—the same memories—over and over again, similar to replaying a tape or reshowing a portion of a movie film. The evidence is that *all* the perceptions we are ever exposed to are stored somewhere in the memory, waiting to be recalled by stress, narcosynthesis, electrical stimulation, or perhaps just a bit of brow-wrinkling.

The discovery that a brain could be frozen and still remember after it had thawed out was a hard blow to the proponents of the "reverberating" or dynamic theory of memory. In fact, with the introduction of the "molecular memory trace" concept, electrical theories in general have for some time taken a back seat. Pushed by men like Hydén and more recently espoused by Jacobson, McConnell, Rosenblatt, and Ungar in the United States, this concept suggests that memory is stored in a molecule, something like the storage, in the DNA of the gene, of the "blueprint" for life. More conservatively, there at least exists a chemical coding analogous to signs posted on a highway to guide the traveler along the proper route.

For ages men have eaten fish as brain food or have devoured tribal chieftains in order to acquire their superior mental powers. Is there an elixir that will give us a superior memory and hence a superior mentality? Years ago glutamic acid was touted as a memory potion but faded from the scientific scene after having apparently been oversold. More recently a trade preparation called *Cylert,* a chemical compound known as magnesium pemoline, was fed to animals and to men and credited with improving memory. So was RNA, the transfer nucleic acid involved in the genetic mechanism. As with glutamic acid, Cylert now also seems to be somewhat discredited, but as it vanished from the journals there came a far more startling claim—it was possible to transfer learning, by chemical means, from one animal to another.

Most remarkable of all, this phenomenon of the transferal of learning has now been demonstrated in laboratories in many countries around the world and is a generally accepted scientific fact. Years ago Jonathan Swift wrote of a "Cephalick tincture" reported by Gulliver, which tincture, when eaten on a wafer, imparted knowledge to schoolboys. As yet, only simple paradigms such as learned responses to sound or light and maze learning have been transferred by today's tinctures. But even this accomplishment is remarkable and encouraging enough to enable researchers to talk of the possibility of "chemical learning" for humans.

This is not to say that the memory experts in search of the "engram" (the name given to the hypothetical impression or trace created by a memory; the mechanism for recall of the memory) have found their quarry. Of all man's scientific tasks, identification of the physical basis of memory may be the most difficult. This task may be, as a number of scientists have suggested, impossible. Mathematician Kurt Gödel advanced a proof to show that there are certain problems unsolvable by a person who is using the system involving those problems. A crude analogy might be the fish who cannot infer the water in which he lives. Some philosophers have held that certain things are, by the

very nature of nature, unknowable. Another difficulty was suc-
cinctly spelled out by psychologist W. C. Corning:

> In the study of brain functions we rely upon a biased, poorly
> understood, and frequently unpredictable organ in order to study
> the properties of another such organ; we have to use a brain to
> study a brain. . . . There is no "super-computer" to which we can
> submit our experimental strategies and theories to determine
> whether we are on the right track. . . .

Despite the dearth of research tools and the lack of a "super-
computer" that would map out the right track, the search goes on.
It is conceivable that one day there will be a great breakthrough
in the field of memory research, a breakthrough of even greater
import than the unleashing of nuclear energy, the entry into the
space age, or the discovery of the DNA molecule structure. For
memory affects intelligence, and once man has discovered the
secrets of memory, he can perhaps improve his memory so that
the average man of tomorrow will be beyond the genius of today.
And who can say how far genius may climb?

Chapter Two

HISTORY OF BRAIN STUDIES

Alfred Russell Wallace, the English naturalist who, contemporaneously with Charles Darwin, published the theory of natural selection, made some interesting observations on man's unique place in the natural world. After human beings had acquired the intellectual and moral faculties that distinguished them from the animals, Wallace wrote, they were then only slightly susceptible to further modifications through natural selection or evolution. Man's brain, rather than changing through evolution, began to dictate the further changes in man. In addition, some scientists theorize, counter to the natural selection view, that man was created much as he is today. From either viewpoint, man's brain raises him loftily above the animals and gives him dominion over the world. In time, man's brain may make him master of himself. Because of human memory, we can trace the long history of man's search for his identity.

Ironically, man's brain had made him the fittest survivor for millions of years before he was even aware of this vital organ. Among the first evidences of man's awareness of the brain were the crude trepanning operations that the Peruvian Indians performed centuries ago. It has been suggested that this pioneer brain surgery might have been of a therapeutic nature, antedating the topectomies and lobotomies of recent years. However, even if primitive surgeons were medically, not superstitiously, motivated, their work was fleeting and not followed up until modern times.

Many early Greek thinkers considered the brain as merely

"that puzzling thing in the head." Aristotle, the great logician, thought of the heart as paramount in reasoning and the brain as simply an organ to cool the blood! Along with emotion, reason was generally believed to be seated in the midsection, the gut of the animal. The Greek word *phren,* for diaphragm, figures in such common words as phrenology, schizophrenia, frenzy, and frantic. Hysteria derives from the Greek word for womb. Human temperament even now may be characterized as choleric, phlegmatic, melancholic, sanguine—referring respectively to disturbances of the gallbladder, general inflammation, excesses of black bile, and blood.

Jan Batista van Helmont, a noted Flemish physician and chemist, performed the first scientific studies in the botanical field, discovered carbon dioxide, and gave us the concept of gasses as a class of matter as well as the word *gas* itself. Yet this seventeenth-century scientist believed that the soul resided in the stomach.

It is incorrect to charge off such erroneous beliefs to silliness, stupidity, or superstition. Even Pavlov used the classification of temperaments mentioned earlier, and psychologists James and Lange produced the well-known theory of stimulus-response, which hinges on a visceral reaction. We cling to the old idea that our center of gravity is somehow also the center of emotion and reason. We still love "with all our hearts," and in the 1964 presidential campaign we were told that "in your heart you know he's right." Today, "gut" methodologies are popular in education, sociology, and other fields.

Before man could begin to study with any accuracy such things as mind and memory, he had to locate those functions physically. That search has been strangely difficult. Despite such clues as head-scratching when faced with a problem requiring thought, ancient mind-seekers complicated the search by looking everywhere but in the head for answers. The philosophy of dualism—the belief in the soul as a separate entity from the mind and body—also deferred the seekers. Dualism stems from early superstition and the belief in spirits. Some ancients believed that when man slept, his ghostlike soul left his body. "Giving up the ghost" was standard terminology in ancient times, and such supernatural notions stood in the way of rational examination of the mind.

Of course, there were some thinkers who did use their heads in the process. Hippocrates, the physician who left us the ethical heritage of the Hippocratic oath, also reasoned acutely as to the function of the brain:

> And men ought to know that from nothing else but from the brain come joys, delights, laughter and sports, and sorrows, griefs, despondency and lamentations. And by the brain in a special manner we acquire wisdom and knowledge, and see and hear, and know what are foul and what are fair, what are bad and what are good, what are sweet and what are unsavory. . . . By the brain we distinguish objects of relish and disrelish; and the same things do not always please us. And by the same organ we become mad and delirious, and fears and terrors assail us, some by night and some by day.

This was four centuries before the birth of Christ.

Another searcher on the right track was Herophilus, a Greek anatomist who worked from 300 B.C. to about 250 B.C. He dissected the bodies of animals and men and was particularly interested in comparisons of their brains. Furthermore, he divided nerves into those that received sensations and those that signaled to the muscles for action, correctly visualizing the sensory inputs and motor outputs of the brain. Erasistratus, a contemporary of Herophilus, defined the cerebrum and the smaller cerebellum, and he believed that the complex convolutions of the human brain coincided with its intellectual superiority over the brains of animals.

In the second century A.D., the philosopher-emperor Marcus Aurelius probed the mind-soul problem and wrote: "Such as are thy habitual thoughts, such also will be the character of thy mind; for the soul is dyed by the thoughts." His court physician was the great Galen, whose research and published works remained the ultimate medical authority until the writings of Andreas Vesalius and William Harvey some 1,400 years later. Galen misinterpreted the significance of the circulation of blood, but he showed that the brain intervenes between the sense organs

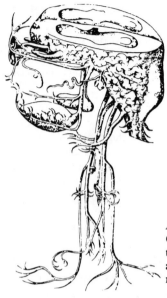

An early drawing by Vesalius, showing Galen's division of the anterior portion of the brain, with sensory nerves attached, and the posterior portion, with motor nerves.

and the muscles. He believed that the brain was also involved in mental processes, and he assigned memory to "animal spirits," a concept that remained in vogue until the time of Descartes.

The Renaissance Brain   More than a millennium passed in the long scientific hiatus known as the Middle Ages. The term "Dark Ages" is seldom honored now because there was much social, business, and literary development during this time. However, the church looked with displeasure on dissection and on attempts to associate the soul with the body. Not until the Renaissance neared, with its Galileos and da Vincis, was the search for man's mind again taken up in an intelligent fashion. Even then scientific inquiry was difficult and fraught with danger, as Galileo learned at his telescope. But inquisitive men persevered, peering inward at man's brain as well as outward into the universe. If anything, the challenge of the inward search was greater.

In 1504 Gregor Reisch published a book, *Margarita Philosophica,* which discussed the brain and which included a diagram of various areas of the brain and the function of these areas. The forebrain he described as a "common sensory" area, connected by nerves to eyes, ears, nose, and tongue. The forebrain was considered the seat of fantasy and imagination. In the midbrain thought and judgment took place, and the hindbrain Reisch held to be where memories were accumulated and stored.

Andreas Vesalius, a Flemish anatomist, was born in 1514. He was keenly interested in dissecting specimens, including the human body, but had to travel to Italy for the freedom he

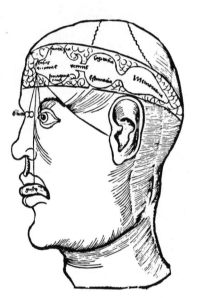

This is how Gregor Reisch visualized the brain in his book, *Margarita Philosophica,* published in 1504. The frontal cavity served as a "common sensorium"; the middle cavity housed thought; and the rearmost was the seat of memory.

needed in his research. His book, *On the Structure of the Human Body,* has been called the first accurate work on anatomy. In it he disagreed completely with the Aristotelian view that the heart was the seat of emotion and mental processes; the brain and its associated nervous system, according to Vesalius, was the true center of these phenomena. It is fitting that at about this same time Copernicus, by locating the sun at the center of our planetary system, dealt a death blow to the proud Ptolemaic theory of earth as the center of that system. Similarly, man's brain was declared the true center of his personal universe.

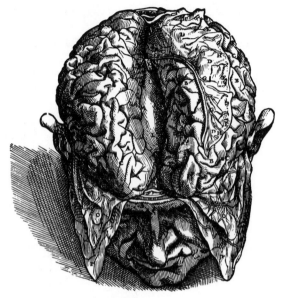

Woodcut from Andreas Vesalius's *De Humani Corporis Fabrica* accurately shows his dissection of the brain.

Vesalius learned that removal of the brain resulted in loss of sensation and movement. He also made this quantitative observation:

> The mass of the brain attains its highest dimensions in man, which we know is the most perfect animal, and that his brain is found to be bigger than that of three oxen; and then in proportion to the size of the body, first the ape, and next the dog exhibit a large brain, suggesting that animals excel in the size of their brains in proportion as they seem the more openly and clearly endowed with the faculties of the chief soul.

Vesalius vindicated with scientific experiments the shrewd guesses of predecessors like Hippocrates. Yet, even though an answer to the question of the location of memory was seemingly close at hand, the mystery only deepened. The brain, it developed, was a most complex organ, comprising a number of identifiable portions, any of which might be the ultimate resting place of the mind.

Cogito, Ergo   René Descartes, philosopher and mathematician, was born in France in 1596. Well known for his
synthesis of algebra and geometry into analytic geometry, Descartes is hailed by some as the father of modern philosophy. It
was Descartes who observed, "Cogito, ergo sum," which means "I
think, therefore I am." Cynics suggest he might better have
stated it as follows: "I think, therefore I *think* I am." Scientist
W. Grey Walter comments, perhaps with tongue in cheek, on the
difference between man and monkey. According to Walter, the
first thought of a slightly inebriated monkey, might be "Sentio,

René Descartes theorized that reflex actions were caused by the passage
through the nerves of "animal spirits" emanating from the brain in
response to sensory stimulation. His book *Traité de l'Homme* was published in 1664, long before discovery of the electrochemical action of the
nervous system.

ergo sum" if he thought in Latin; or, in English, "I feel, therefore I am." Walter adds that the monkey's *first* thought might be
a besotted human's *last* thought before passing out.
    Semantics aside, Descartes did much more than think on paper
in Latin. He also analyzed the human body in strictly mechanistic terms, seeing it as a living machine of levers, pumps, and

other mechanical devices. He analyzed the thinking process, too, but here he made mistakes. The mind was separate from the body, he declared, adhering to the traditional dualistic view. And it was the pineal gland rather than the brain itself that mediated between the supernatural mind and the natural body. He selected this tiny organ because he thought it existed only in man. However, it *does* exist in other animals, as scientists have since learned.

Perhaps it was Descartes's deep religious conviction that made him cling to the concept of a separate mind. It is interesting to note that he was working on an extension of the Copernican theory when he heard that Galileo had been condemned as a heretic. Descartes promptly discarded his scientific approach and evolved a ridiculous but expedient theory that left the earth as the center of our planetary system.

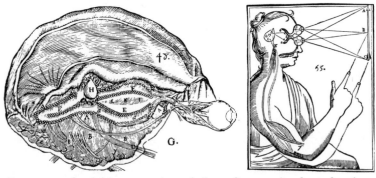

Descartes refined his conception of the reflex arc in these drawings. Incorrectly, he assigned the pineal body the function of mediating action between sensory nerves and motor nerves. What he called the "pores" of the nerves we would call synapses.

Despite his mystical mistake-making, Descartes added valuable insights to the theory of the mind. He suggested the mechanism of nerves, for example, and described what is now called reflex action. Descartes also spoke of a man's experiences leading to the extension of what he called "pores" in the brain, a curious but crudely analogous parallel to the process now believed to occur.

Descartes died of pneumonia after a winter of service in Sweden as court philosopher to Queen Christina. Strangely, his head was kept in that foreign land when his body was sent home, and it was not returned until many years later.

This was the age of Shakespeare, and the bard reflected the emerging scientific sentiment of his time when he described the brain as that organ "which some suppose the soul's frail dwellinghouse." And who but a scientist-poet could conceive the following lines in "Love's Labor Lost"?

> These are begot in the ventricle of memory, nourished in the womb of pia mater, and delivered upon the mellowing of occasion.

This was the age of Thomas Hobbes, too, and that great philosopher challenged Descartes's belief in a supernatural mind or soul. Thought, said Hobbes, was natural and physical, as mechanistic in function as the body that Descartes had described. Hobbes had more courage than his idea had success, but it would persevere until others could establish its validity in later years.

Even scientific facts are not always as obvious as they seem, a thought Karl Lashley may have had in mind when he wrote his book *Why the Brain Is in the Head.* However, centuries of detective work by many mind-seekers had at last established the facts that the mind *was* located in the head and that the brain was indeed the seat of reason. But the mind, like the atom, is made up of different parts with different properties. Once they located the mind in the head, scientists turned to the question of the location of memory. Thomas Willis, an English physician and pioneer investigator of the brain, began to zero in on the site of memory in his book, *Cerebri Anatome,* printed in 1664. Arguing with those who thought memory was housed in the cerebellum, he declared that it was in the cerebrum, or roof, which covers the rest of the organ. He used an appealing, homely argument for his case:

> The ancients offered nothing on the general function and use of the cerebellum worthy of its craftsmanship or suited to its structure. Some have decided that it is another cerebrum and performs the same actions as that; but if anyone were to be provided with

a fool's soft cerebrum, I very much doubt that he would become wise if he were to obtain a harder and more solid cerebellum. Some locate memory in this place, supposing the cerebellum to be like a chest or repository in which the idea or image of things already recognized may be preserved separately from newly entering appearances; but it is far more likely that this faculty resides in the cortical gyri of the cerebrum (as we demonstated elsewhere), for as often as we attempt to remember something long past we rub our temples and the forepart of our head; we arouse the cerebrum and stir up the indwelling spirits as if busily seeking to pluck out something lying hidden there; meanwhile we attempt nothing at the rear of the head, nor are we conscious of any movement there. Furthermore, we have demonstrated that phantasy and imagination act in the cerebrum, but memory so depends upon imagination that its action seems to be reflective or inverted. Therefore it is necessary that memory be located in the same cloister, that is, in the cerebrum, for it is very clear that there is no direct communication between the cerebrum and cerebellum.

Although Willis made errors and optimistically jumped far ahead of scientific verification, scientists have now conceded the validity of his hypothesis that memory resides in the cerebrum, or cerebral cortex. Once the island of reason had been found, the searchers of old were succeeded by anatomists who specialized in mapping out the mind. But the charts were marked *unknown* in the areas of memory. How, with the keenest scalpel or strongest microscope, does one uncover the abstract treasure of a lifetime of experiences?

The Anatomy of Memory   Albrecht Von Haller, a Swiss physiologist born in 1708, was the first to show that all nerves led either to the brain or to the spinal cord and that the nerves, rather than muscles or other tissues, were the instruments of sensation and response. Haller said that the medulla was the source of sensation and movement. Beyond that, however, he was scientifically cautious: "Our present knowledge does not permit us to speak with any show of truth about the more complicated functions of the mind or to assign in the brain to imagination its seat, to common sensation its seat, to memory its seat."

Jean Lamarck was a French naturalist born in 1744. At the Museum of Natural History in Paris, he carried on the uncompleted work of Linnaeus in classifying the invertebrates. In addition, he delved into the question of evolution and produced a theory concerning acquired characteristics that was later eclipsed by the natural selection theories of Darwin and Wallace. Lamarck extended his theory of acquired characteristics to include the brain. He believed that experiences left memory traces like etchings on the "organ of intelligence." Here he was on firmer ground.

In 1749 David Hartley published *Observations on Man, His Frame, His Duty and His Expectations,* a "doctrine of mechanism" that was the clearest and most accurate statement of brain function up to that time and perhaps for another two centuries. Without the benefit of high-power microscopes or a knowledge of living cells and the electrochemical nature of life, Hartley nevertheless saw with exciting clarity how the brain functions. The workings of the mind he envisioned as deriving from "vibrations" of the brain itself. In addition, there were finer movements, called "vibratiuncles," for the subtle shadings of intelligence. Hartley also investigated and described a theory of the association of ideas, a theory that still holds up well today.

With dissection of the brain came the realization that there are certain landmarks generally evident on all brains, even though individual brains vary one from another as faces do. Early anatomists began to carve up and to map the brain and thus to assure themselves immortality in the annals of medicine. The seventeenth-century French anatomist, Franciscus de le Doe Sylvius, is remembered for the Sylvian fissure. The great central fissure separating the two hemispheres is called the Rolandic fissure. The resulting lobes drew less glamorous names, such as frontal, for the obvious reason, and parietal, temporal and occipital for those lobes underlying the skull bones of the same names.

Franz Joseph Gall, born in 1758, was a German physician who became interested in the nerves and the brain. He theorized that the gray matter of the brain was the active portion and that the white matter served as connective tissue. Gall believed that the various portions of the brain controlled various parts of the body; furthermore, he felt that brain shape correlated with emotion and temperament. Extending this argument, he assumed that the shape of the brain affected the shape of the protective skull. An expert, therefore, could infer all manner of facts about an individual from examining the bumps on his head. Here was the beginning of the pseudoscience phrenology.

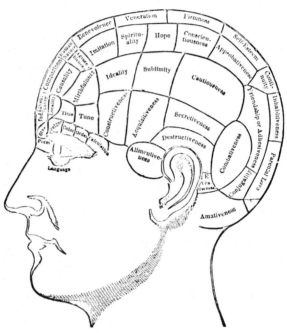

Gall's phrenology inevitably led to such extremes as this diagram of the "phrenological organs," including such areas as "Friendship or Adhesiveness" and "Conjugality."

Phrenologists hinted enough at the truth to make this pastime a dangerous one, because characterizing a man from his cranial contours is about as scientific as characterizing him from his fingerprints. A convenient similarity exists, though, in the fact that a man's cerebral cortex, his so-called "gray matter," is perhaps as unique as his fingerprints. Although all of us have brains of roughly the same structure, no two are any more alike than are two sets of fingerprints.

Although phrenology has been exploited in a most unscientific manner, Gall's basic assumption about localized, specialized control areas in the brain was correct, and later work by other scientists strengthened his theory. For example, a Parisian doctor, Marc Dax, found that when strokes paralyzed the right side of a

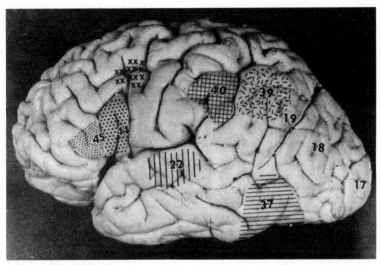

"Mapped" areas of the human brain, based on the system of the physiologist K. Brodmann in 1925. Areas 17, 18, and 19 are the areas of vision and visual association; 22 is audition and speech; 39 and 40 are sensory integration; 44 is speech.

right-handed person, the victim usually suffered some loss of speech, also. Being aware of the crossover of control from one hemisphere of the brain to the opposite side of the body, Dax decided that control of speech must lie in the left hemisphere of the brain.

The Frenchman Paul Broca was the first modern surgeon to perform trepanning operations (of course, if one assumes that the ancients had really performed this operation for surgical reasons, Broca was not the first). In 1861 Broca demonstrated conclusively that damage to the third convolution of the left frontal lobe of the brain caused aphasia, the loss of speaking ability. Within two decades this mapping-out process had been extended to much more of the cerebrum and showed that certain areas in the brain controlled certain bodily functions.

Elaborating on these beginning attempts at mapping the functions of the brain, the English neurologist Hughlings Jackson pinned down and defined the work of several other areas of the brain. The sensory functions of the brain were accomplished behind the central fissures in the lobes of both hemispheres; motor functions took place in front of these fissures. Jackson announced his findings a century ago, just after the end of the Civil War in America.

For all the investigative work that had been done and all the great discoveries of what man harbored beneath his tough skull, little if anything was known of the actual mechanism of the brain. What was a memory? How did man learn? The first glimmers appeared in a Russian laboratory, and the subject was not man but man's best friend, the dog.

Pavlov and His Dog Ivan Petrovich Pavlov was born in 1849 in Ryazan, Russia. He studied natural science and after receiving his doctorate performed, with dogs, experiments that demonstrated the action of the autonomic nervous system with respect to digestion. For this work Pavlov received the Nobel Prize in medicine in 1904. His work on digestion interested him in doing further study in reflexes. Again using dogs as subjects, Pavlov was able to produce "conditioned reflexes" in these animals. A conditioned reflex is a form of learning, in contrast to the "unconditioned reflex" or automatic response.

Pavlov was one of the first to conduct scientific experiments on the learning process; these experiments, of course, encompassed the workings of the brain and of memory. However, Pavlov was mainly interested in the "what" of the process rather than in the "how." Results were paramount to Pavlov, and he was content to let the brain and its memory mechanism remain a mysterious black box for others to probe. His work laid the foundation for

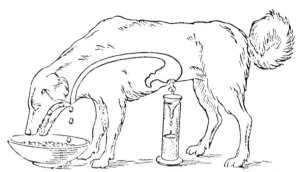

Pavlov's experiments with conditioned reflexes were conducted mainly on dogs. This diagram shows the salivation and secretion of digestive juices that occur as an unconditioned response. Pavlov linked them to the ringing of a bell and thus created a conditioned response.

the behaviorist school of psychology led by William James, John Broadus Watson, and other Americans.

As we shall see in a later chapter, however, Pavlov did advance a theory of learning based on the network of nerves established by electrical waves generated in the brain as a result of the conditioning process. His suggestion was understandable, for the mysterious electrical force operating in humans had been known to scientists for approximately a century before Pavlov conducted his experiments.

Fifty years after David Hartley boldly suggested the "vibratory" mechanism of the brain, an Italian named Luigi Galvani discovered the motive force of these vibrations and "vibratiuncles." As is often the case with a major scientific discovery, Galvani stumbled onto "animal electricity" by accident and then completely misinterpreted his findings. Studying the nerves of frogs, he noted an unexplainable twitching in the leg of a dead specimen strung on a wire. Investigation convinced Galvani that his initial conclusion—that atmospheric electricity was motivating the muscles—was wrong, and that it was the muscles themselves that generated the electricity. A countryman named Alessandro Volta ridiculed Galvani's findings and "proved" his point by generating electricity without the atmosphere and without living tissue. He used a "cell" of metals instead and thus created the first electric battery.

In the politics of Italian science, Galvani lost the battle of "animal electricity," and his brilliant discovery was sidetracked for some time while scientists in many countries worked on artificial electricity. Michael Faraday introduced the induction coil to science before the middle of the nineteenth century, and the coil was in turn introduced into electrophysiological laboratories by Dubois-Reymond. A physiologist named Biedermann also published a two-volume work titled *Electrophysiology*. However, little work of a concrete nature was done for some time with the new tool for research of living matter.

The Electrochemical Brain   Just where the notorious hypnotist Dr. Anton Mesmer fits into the search for the mind is hard to determine definitely. In his paper on the discovery of "animal magnetism," Mesmer told of effecting marvelous mental cures by simply laying on his hands. Although he did experiment in seances with magnetism and static electricity, he claimed that he dropped this approach as early as 1776. This was the year of the signing of the Declaration of Independence, and one of the framers of that document, Benjamin Franklin, served on a scientific investigation team that thoroughly discredited Mesmer and his theory of animal magnetism.

Electrophysiology surfaced again in 1870. Strangely, the location was the battlefield at Sedan, which was littered with war dead. The researchers were two Prussian doctors, Fritsch and Hitzig, who were aware of the strange experiments of Galvani and others. They applied electric currents to the exposed brains of the dead soldiers, and among their findings was the fact that stimulation of the right hemisphere of the brain resulted in immediate twitching of the opposite side of the body.

Electrophysiologists corroborated Hughlings Jackson's localization of motor and sensory areas, too. Stimulation of the frontal lobes of the left hemisphere caused a movement in the right legs of the subjects; electrical prodding of the back of the brain brought no similar motor response. However, even though electricity could actuate the nervous system, there was still no proof that the brain itself operated electrically. Not until 1875 did an English physician, R. Caton, discover that the brain itself produced tiny amounts of electricity—just as Galvani had insisted in 1795. Thus it was less than a century ago that man established that the driving force of his brain was an electrochemical one.

In our electronic age it is hard to conceive of a scientific laboratory equipped with only crude batteries and coils and harder still to conceive of men investigating bioelectricity with such crude equipment. Willem Einthoven, a Dutch physiologist enamored of Galvani's provocative findings, did much to refine the detection and measurement of living electricity. Einthoven developed the "string galvanometer," a delicate thread conducting an electrical current through a magnetic field. Two American physiologists, Joseph Erlanger and Herbert Gasser, improved the new measuring device and, like Einthoven, performed many experiments with nerves. Einthoven, in 1924, and Erlanger and Gasser, in 1944, received Nobel Prizes for their research findings.

In 1906 Einthoven produced electrocardiograms and correlated them with heart disorders. Other physiologists began to investigate the electrical discharges in the brain, which were much weaker but which were still electricity. In 1913 Prawdwicz-Neminski made "electrocerebrograms" of a dog, a tracing we now call an electroencephalograph.

In 1928 research and development of electrical instruments had advanced to the point where Hans Berger was measuring brain waves with a technique known as electroencephalography. Within several years the "Berger rhythm" was well known in the neurological world. Berger developed his technique for recording brain waves from the older electrocardiograph method, in which the stronger electrical output of the heart was measured with electrodes, much as one would check a battery.

Berger's work with electroencephalograms was extended considerably by English researchers, including Lord Adrian at Cambridge and Dr. W. Grey Walter (born in America) at the Burden Neurological Institute in Bristol, England.

The most prominent pattern in the electrical activity of the brain is called the alpha rhythm, characteristic of a person at rest and with his eyes closed. This rhythm is quite slow for an elec-

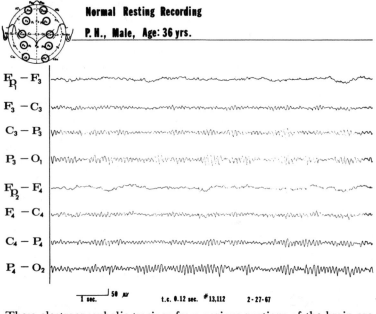

These electroencephalic tracings from various portions of the brain are keyed to the diagram of the head shown above.

trical frequency, about 10 cycles per second. Berger thought that this activity emanated from the whole brain. However, Adrian and an assistant named Matthews showed that the alpha rhythm came instead from the visual association areas in the occipital lobe. Today the alpha rhythm is thought to be located primarily in the parieto-occipital region.

Other rhythms were also discovered, including a beta rhythm at from 14 to 30 cycles per second, a delta rhythm from 0.5 to 13 cycles per second, and a theta rhythm from 4 to 7 cycles per second. The amplitude, or strength, of the electrical rhythms is very small and ranges from about 5 millionths of a volt to 50 millionths of a volt, the higher figure generally found in children.

The Lobotomists   Quite naturally the activity of the brain began to be treated as a purely electrical phenomenon. Lord Sherrington, one of the pioneers of neurophysiology, had referred most poetically to the brain as an "enchanted loom where millions of flashing shuttles weave a dissolving pattern, always a meaningful pattern though never an abiding one." For all the great interest in the electrical bases of memory, however, physiologists continued the earlier surgical approaches. The techniques of Broca were improved and extended.

The English doctor, Thomas Willis, had pointed to man's scratching of the forward portion of his head when he was trying to remember something. Others adopted this approach and assigned the memory function to the frontal lobes of the brain. However, in the middle of the nineteenth century a Vermont man suffered accidental damage to his frontal lobes with no apparent loss of memory or skill—only his personality seemed to change. In 1933 John Fulton and Carlyle Jacobsen at the Yale Medical School removed prefrontal lobes from two chimpanzees, and the results paralleled the experience of the Vermont man. By 1935 Drs. Egaz Moniz and Almeida Lima in Portugal were performing prefrontal lobotomies on hopeless mental patients. The frontal lobes were severed from the rest of the brain, and the operation seemed to lessen the terrible anxiety the subjects suffered. Their memories seemed unaffected. In time, however, scientists found that the imaginative processes of those who underwent lobotomy suffered greatly.

Bare Beginning   In more than two thousand years, then, only a handful of researchers have sought the "frail dwellinghouse of the mind." Slowly they narrowed the hunting grounds, eliminating false leads with great difficulty. They have finally established the brain as the site of mind and memory, but the end is still not in sight. Like the atoms of Democritus, the brain is proving to be divisible almost *ad infinitum*. In three pounds of pinkish jelly, the seekers of the mind have found something that seems to defy final solution. How, they ask, can the immortality of man be plucked from this double handful of nervous tissue? How, even with the most powerful of microscopes, can it be proved that Hobbes and others are right, that consciousness, imagination, memory, and all the rest, can be spelled out by a handful of neurons?

Man has cooled substances to within a tantalizing fraction of a degree from "absolute zero," that total lack of temperature at which point all motion is thought to cease, but he cannot achieve that last tiny thermal distance. Man has split the atom and probed its nucleus, only to find particles within particles. And so it is with the brain, at which we shall now look more closely.

Chapter Three

MAN'S BRAIN

Man's mind, as we have seen, was once held to be in his heart, his stomach, or elsewhere, and many a youngster has a misconception about the "seat of learning" as a result of the paddling he might receive for failing in the classroom. It is now well established, however, that mental phenomena are primarily functions of the brain. Consciousness and thinking processes reside in the "wonderful raveled knot" on top of man's spine, and we must look for their mechanism in the cellular structure and organization of this marvelous organ.

The paramecium hasn't a brain in its head, the good reason being that it doesn't have a head. This one-celled creature, capable of responding meaningfully to its environment, is a model of simplicity in a living thing. Sherrington and others have said that the paramecium "learns." However, without losing sight of the miracle that nature accomplished in forming the living cell, we can nevertheless see that unicellular life is a far cry from the sophisticated multicellular organism we call man. The cell gets along without a brain much as Robinson Crusoe got along without a government—the cell neither needs nor can provide a brain. Only with the development of multicellular organisms and the specialization of individual cells to perform tasks more efficiently did centralized sensory and response switchboards evolve.

Organ of Survival   Unicellular creatures can, in theory, live forever because the cell need not die. Ironically, in achieving a brain, life gave up its earlier immortality. With multicellular beings came differentiation among and specialization of various cells, and with multicellular beings came death, also. The primitive organism, volvox, is a classic example. Volvox, a cluster of cells shaped into a sphere, harbors within itself "daughter cells" that at birth kill the parent organism. Another example is man's inability to replace lost limbs as can a lesser being like the salamander. The salamander's cells lack the high state of specialization found in man but can repeat the original process of budding and growth to provide replacement limbs. Worms do even better, growing whole new creatures from each of the pieces into which they are cut. Here we had better end the analogies because, as we shall see in a later chapter, the planarian, a flatworm, has a brain that some scientists credit with miraculous properties of memory.

The brain in any creature is basically an organ of survival, the principal organ of the nervous system. Nerve tissue is one of the four primary tissues of the body; the other three are epithelium, muscle, and connective tissue. Even such a primitive life form as the amoeba needs to be aware of the outside world and needs to carry messages so that it can properly respond to its environment and thus stay alive. Nervous tissue can carry messages relating to pressure, light, sound, smell, and other stimuli. Nerves can also work in the opposite direction—with control signals. Light strikes a plant; as its nervous system becomes aware of the light, petals open or close, depending on the survival needs of the plant.

In primitive organisms nerve responses are autonomous, or self-governed. A part of man's nervous system functions in this way, automatically and with no conscious awareness or effort. Breathing, digestion, and such reflex responses as reaction to being stuck with a pin are examples. But even a worm, as we have noted, needs a central switchboard to process and to act upon nerve signals. In a worm the "brain" is more properly called a cephalic ganglion. A ganglion is a mass of nerve cells, a knot of tissue or "nerve network."

Nerve Networks   A sponge is a primitive, multicellular animal and does not have a true nervous system. However, even in protozoa, which are unicellular creatures, "action potentials" or electrochemical changes accompany the movement of tentacles. These action potentials are transmitted from cell to cell of the sponge through a process called neuroid transmission, a forerunner of the true nervous system. For example, poking a sponge with a pin results in the closing of openings in its structure. As we move up the evolutionary scale, we find crude nervous systems in the invertebrates and more refined ones in the vertebrates.

The forerunner of the brain was the simple "nerve net" or network of nerves in the invertebrates, which are creatures without spines. The jellyfish provides an example of this kind of communication method. In the unicellular amoeba there is nothing to connect. A two-celled creature requires two connections. From this point, however, the number of "wires" increases much faster than the simple one-to-one correspondence required for the two-celled creature. Three nerves linked to each other yield six connections, five give 20 connections, and 100 nerves tied together in a network produce 9900 connections. It is little wonder that soon these networks began to clump together into ganglia. This was the solution that insects evolved to the problem of communication and control.

Because the ganglia in the forward or head end of an organism are generally the most bombarded with environmental signals, these ganglia become relay centers. Rather than have all of a creature's feet or the tentacles of a worm respond individually, nature evolved a central control system in the head so that, for example, the limbs would operate in unison to produce better locomotion.

Later came the process of storing information and correlating various kinds of incoming messages from the outside world with that information. Here was the first crude glimmer of the brain, an outgrowth of the primitive survival mechanism of the cell.

The beginnings of a brain are seen in the "notochord." The tiny lancet (a small marine creature that burrows in the sand of warm, shallow water) is an example and has been called a bridge between invertebrate and vertebrate creatures. The lancet possesses a stiff neural cord that runs the length of its soft body and that is capped at the head end with a knot of nerves or ganglion that may be dignified with the term "budding brain."

Life began in the sea, and it is not surprising that a fish called the lamprey was first to develop a true brain. This development is thought to have taken some billion years after the appearance of the first protozoa. Man's different responses to the same signals from sensory organs are succinct statements of his mental superiority; however, this sophistication of choice came slowly. Today we can still see the primitive reactions of the sea anemone, a simple marine animal readily observed in tidal pools. The closing of its tentacles around potential food is a reflex action to certain stimuli. However, continued feeding changes the response, and much as we do, the anemone pushes away food when full. In the anemone this change in response cannot be attributed to a brain but to the sense organs themselves through a process called accommodation or adaptation. Only when there is a permanent change in the ganglial structure because of experience is there true learning, and such changes do occur in life forms as low as worms.

Although the flatworm does have a brain that controls its swimming motions, part of the learning of the flatworm seems to reside elsewhere than in the brain. If the head is cut off, for example, the worm grows a new head that retains the prior learning. In the bilaterally symmetrical vertebrates, however, the brain becomes dominant in controlling responses to the environment.

Having traced the growth of the brain from the action potential in single cells through neuroid transmission of the sponge and the head ganglia in slightly higher life forms, we move on to the brain most meaningful to us, that found in vertebrate forms, the highest of which is man himself. Intervening developments occurred, however. The dinosaur Diplodocus, a quadruped vegetarian, was an interesting specimen from the standpoint of its brain—or brains, rather. The beast was some 80 feet in length and, perhaps because of the problem in communicating information from one end to the other, had one brain in its tiny head and a second in the pelvic area. As the *Chicago Tribune* eulogized Diplodocus:

> You will observe by the remains
> The creature had two sets of brains . . .
> If something slipped his forward mind
> 'Twas rescued by the one behind.
> One in his head, the usual place,
> The other at the spinal base.
> Thus he could reason *a priori*
> As well as *a posteriori.*

Here was the development of ganglia into two brains, but this approach was not pursued by nature. Instead, cephalic ganglia developed into a single brain at the head end of the creature.

The Human Brain   The growth of a human from a fertilized egg cell is an awesome phenomenon. And surely the development of the brain from a microscopic bit of tissue—the neural plate—is the most miraculous part of that growth. From the neural plate comes a neural tube, which develops rapidly as ectodermal or skin cells elongate and divide by the growth process known as mitosis. From this neural tube comes not only the brain but also the spinal cord and the entire nervous system.

Cell division doubles the number of cells with each splitting. One cell splits into two, two into four, and four into eight—not impressive thus far. But there is a legend about a hero who was promised his reward in grains of wheat, one on the first square of the chess board, two on the second square, and so on. To the dismay of the king who made the pledge, this reward would have totaled 18,446,744,073,709,551,615 grains of wheat by the sixty-fourth square—enough to cover the entire earth with wheat to a depth of one inch! Human growth does not require sixty-four cell divisions; however, there are enough divisions so that some 50 trillion cells result, including ten billion neurons in the brain.

The neuroblasts, which are the precursors of brain cells, mul-

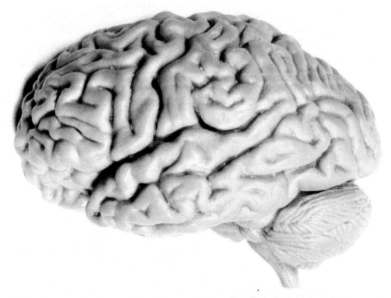

The human brain: pictured are various lobes of the cerebrum and cerebellum and, in addition, the brain stem.

tiply so rapidly from the original neural plate that about six months after conception the fetal brain comprises nearly all the ten billion neurons. However, the cells are nowhere near full size; in fact, they weigh only about three ounces, compared with the three pounds that the adult brain weighs. At birth, weight has increased to ten or twelve ounces, and by age six the brain weighs about 95 per cent of the weight at maturity; maximum growth is attained about age twenty.

At birth, man's brain is growing fastest; however, mental development differs greatly among the animals. For example, although the pig is a brain developer on a par with man, the guinea pig is far more precocious and is able to fend for itself quite well a few hours after birth. Rats, on the other hand, are even slower to develop their brains than man, with most of the growth coming after birth. Even among men, there is some difference in brain development at birth. African and Central and South American babies are ahead of European babies by as much as six to eight weeks with respect to brain development. This difference, however, is not an indicator of ultimate potential in the brain department and the slower developers usually make up for any early differences.

Man's adult brain weight of about three pounds represents only about 2 per cent of his total weight, an added tribute to the importance of the organ. Man has a brain heavier than that of huge Diplodocus of old and exceeded today only by the dolphin, the elephant, and the sperm whale. When brain weight is taken as a proportion of total weight, however, man puts the elephant and the whale to shame. Yet the dolphin, gorilla, and mouse all have ratios that compare favorably with that of man. Brain weight in proportion to total weight is not the whole story, either. Although the dolphin and the gorilla are obviously quite intelligent, the former particularly so if the studies of Dr. John Lilly and others are accurate indicators, the mouse hardly qualifies as a creature of high intelligence.

The neural plate, then, grows from microscopic and deceptive simplicity into a complex collection of readily distinguishable

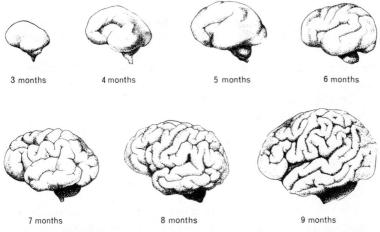

| 3 months | 4 months | 5 months | 6 months |

| 7 months | 8 months | 9 months |

Diagrams of development of the human brain. General shape is defined by three months, and by six months all neurons are present. At birth, brain is well developed with respect to lobes and convolutions of the cortex but weighs only about one-fourth of its adult weight.

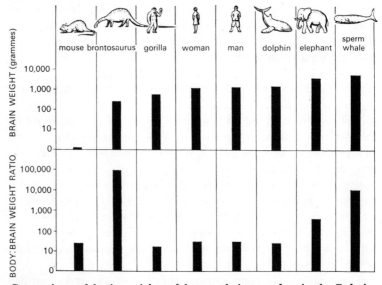

Comparison of brain weights of human beings and animals. Relative weights obviously don't tell the whole story, for top and bottom charts show little difference in gorilla, man, and dolphin.

components in the completely developed brain. We will consider the components in the order in which they develop in the embryo. The first three divisions are known as forebrain, midbrain, and hindbrain, a rather unimaginative set of descriptives. The physiologist dresses them up with the words *prosencephalon, mesencephalon,* and *rhombencephalon,* Latin and Greek terms that mean the same as the English terms.

As the embryo becomes fully developed, the forebrain and the hindbrain subdivide further and acquire new names—*telencephalon, diencephalon, metencephalon,* and *myelencephalon.* These areas subdivide further and produce in the adult brain expansions of the basic structures.

The telencephalon branches into the two cerebral hemispheres, those centers of reason that dominate the brain—and in turn the entire being. From the telencephalon also come the *rhinencephalon,* the olfactory centers of the brain, and certain other centers that are not so easy to categorize. The diencephalon expands into the *thalamus, hypothalamus,* portions of the eyes, and part of the pituitary gland. The metencephalon develops dorsally, or rearward, into the *cerebellum,* the center of muscular coordination. And the myelencephalon becomes the *medulla oblongata*—massive fibers that connect the higher brain centers with the spinal cord.

Each part of the brain is important even though surgeons can completely remove some areas without killing the patient. But the cerebral cortex, the great "roof brain" that completely covers

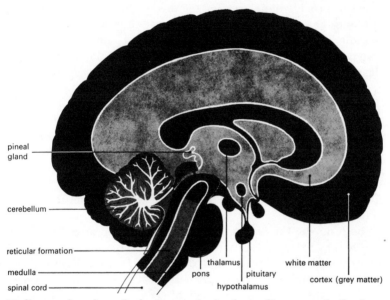

pineal
gland

cerebellum

reticular formation

medulla

spinal cord

thalamus
pons   pituitary
hypothalamus

white matter

cortex (grey matter)

Median section through the human brain shows diagrammatically the major features. The cerebrum is incompletely divided into two halves, with a covering of gray matter and a central mass of white matter. The most highly developed functions of the nervous system, such as remembering and intelligence, are dependent on the cerebrum. The thalamus processes signals from all the sensory systems. The midbrain contains the major nonvisual inputs and output pathways of the cerebrum. The cerebellum controls balance and the precision of voluntary movement. The medulla contains lower centers for sensory and motor functions and, with the hypothalamus, controls heart beats, breathing rates, and digestion.

the structure from which it grew, controls the higher activities of the brain—thinking, judgment, speech, and so on. One writer has aptly compared the cortex to a holding corporation that integrates and extends the services of lesser companies with offices downstairs in the same building. It has been pointed out that if man were equipped only with the so-called old brain, he would have a head about the size of a baseball and would be about as intelligent as that appearance would suggest.

The two cerebral hemispheres are composed of a pinkish-gray mass of tissue, creased and recreased, folded and refolded on itself to provide more area for the myriad connections within it. Joining the two hemispheres is the great cerebral commissure, a bundle of fibers that link the nerve cells of one hemisphere to those of the other and that apparently assist in the sophisticated learning and memory processes of which the brain is capable.

In addition to the wrinkles that convolute the cortex, greater fissures divide the hemispheres into various lobes, just as the Grand Canyon carves up the terrain. These are the earlier mentioned fissures of Rolando, Sylvius, and Broca and the frontal, temporal, parietal, and occipital lobes. The cortex gets its name from the Latin word for tree bark; it is indeed the covering of the cerebrum, with a thickness of about an eighth of an inch. If the cortex were flattened out, it would be about equal in area to a newspaper page.

Both during the development of the fetus and after birth, the brain is guarded zealously to protect it. Even when the body is starved and near the point of death, the brain is "spared," as scientists would state. In experiments adult rats have been starved to death, at which point body weight is reduced to about half the normal weight. Yet the brain of the animal loses no weight at all!

Man is well known as a hardheaded animal. Whether the worm has no skull because he has little brain to protect or has little brain because he has no skull is a moot point. Man, a vertebrate, does have bone in addition to flesh and uses that bone in its strongest forms to protect his most delicate and vital organ.

The heart and lungs are surrounded by the rib cage and are

protected to some extent by the spine. The stomach, liver, and kidneys get little protection and, as a result, suffer frequent harm. Only the brain is encased in armor and, in addition, hermetically sealed in fluid to guard against damage from outside physical blows. Man often adds an artificial helmet to increase his head protection, but nature alone does an admirable job in this respect. Not only is the fragile pink jelly protected from harm, it is also cushioned in fluid to keep even the skull itself from actual contact. In addition to this shock-absorbing fluid are the layers of special membranes that guard against abrasions, the *dura mater* and the *pia mater* (the tough skin and the gentle skin, as the Latin words indicate). Between these layers is the thinner *arachnoid,* Greek for cobweb! Man's brain is thus cradled in a more protective manner than his body was in the womb.

Functions of the Brain   Because a brain worthy of the name appears only in bilaterally symmetrical creatures, it is not surprising that there are, in effect, two brains. The existence of two brains is a survival mechanism, just as two kidneys, two lungs, two eyes, and two ears increase their possessor's chances of staying alive despite injury. There are two hemispheres in the brain, each controlling half of the body. As we mentioned before, the right hemisphere controls the left side; the left hemisphere, the right side. Various explanations for this arrangement have been advanced. One interesting suggestion is that a man who is fighting with a weapon in his right hand will expose the right side of his body—and head—to the enemy. If his head is injured on the right side, he will still be able to fight with his right hand because the uninjured left hemisphere will continue to control his right side. Of course, animals, who don't carry weapons, also have this system of cross control.

The hemispheres are mirror images of each other, each with a full complement of sensory and motor activity centers. Each hemisphere seems capable of taking over complete control of the body, if necessary. Both hemispheres link up at the bottom with the spinal cord, but they are connected in other ways, too. The cerebrum is joined by many bundles of nerve fibers that link like areas. Of these bundles the largest is called the great cerebral commissure, or *corpus callosum,* which contains most of the nerve connections between the hemispheres.

Researchers have proved that the great commissure can be severed with little or no noticeable mental change in the subject. In fact, in rare cases an individual is born with no great commissure. What then is the purpose of the commissure? Surgeons sometimes cut the *corpus callosum* to prevent epilepsy from spreading from the damaged hemisphere to the good one, and Warren McCulloch at Yale University School of Medicine ironically suggested that the commissure serves only to transmit epileptic seizures from one hemisphere to the other. Karl Lashley of Yerkes Laboratory commented that the *corpus callosum* served as a mechanical stiffener to keep the brain hemispheres from "sagging."

Experiments with animals, and to a lesser extent with human beings, have shown that separation of the hemispheres results in the subject's having two separate brains, each capable of learning and retaining knowledge but unable to transmit knowledge to the other brain. Here is a true split personality—the right brain does not know what the left is up to.

Memory apparently can be acquired by both hemispheres at once or by only one; in the latter situation, the one hemisphere will later make the memory trace available on demand to the other hemisphere by means of the connecting nerve links in the great commissure. The purpose of the two hemispheres is not clearly understood. Whether nature provided them simply for the safeguard of a spare brain or because two brains are better than one in problem-solving is difficult to answer.

We have mentioned the division of work among the parts of the brain. Sensory inputs come into the rear portions of the brain; motor activity stems from the forward portions. The brainstem and cerebellum provide the muscular coordination needed in motor activity; the thalamus helps the cortex to integrate sensory messages; the limbic system contributes to emotional experience. The brain is also the seat of the basic drives. Skillful research has identified areas in the brain that seem to control these emotions and drives. The hypothalamus, for example, controls hunger and thirst as well as the sex drive. There are both positive and negative drive areas. The hypothalamic area also controls the emotions of fear and aggressiveness. And there is a "pleasure" center or centers in the brain. When rats were fitted with electrodes that stimulated these areas,

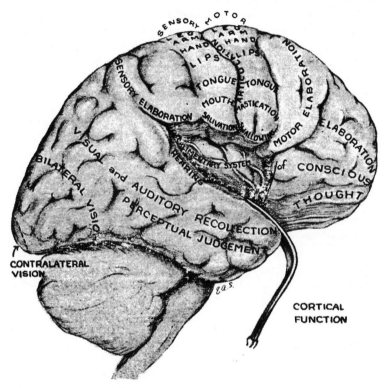

Functions of the various areas of the brain, as diagrammed by Wilder Penfield.

they deliberately pushed a button that administered a pleasurable electric shock thousands of times in rapid succession. Even hunger and the sex urge were forgotten in this orgy of self-administered pleasure.

Primitive brains developed with particular orientation to the sensory inputs of the possessor of the brain. The brain of the fish, for example, is oriented toward olfactory input signals. Other primitive brains favor tactile sensory input, still others the visual or auditory senses. Part of the brain is given over to visceral, or gut, responses—an understandable situation. And, not surprisingly, part of the brain is a somatic map of a man's body.

In the somatic sensory and motor area of the brain, scientists visualize the images projected by neuron networks as those of a tiny man—"a grotesque and somewhat dismembered miniature of the human body." Just as the projection in the brain of a pig

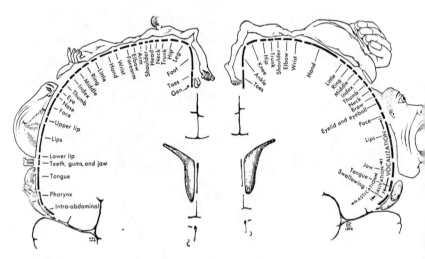

Relative representation of sensory homunculus, left, and motor homunculus, right, in the brain.

is mostly snout because smell is the animal's most meaningful sensory contact with the outside world, and in the brain of a dog is mostly nose, in man the projection is also distorted because hands and fingers are represented as much larger than feet because the former are used more. The lips loom larger than life; in fact, they appear larger than the rest of the head; arms and legs are shown joined; no torso is evident; the head is visualized as separate from the body, and the tongue in turn is separate from the head.

In the rat the scientist finds a somatic map quite similar to the creature itself, with some distortion of the head and lips because most of the senses are located in that area. The monkey understandably has a brain picture that is mostly tail because that appendage is so important in locomotion.

We can trace the evolution of man to some extent in the development of the human embryo, and there is much in the brain of man today that is apparently vestigial. The pineal gland, or pineal body, is a case in point. An outgrowth of the diencephalon, as noted earlier, the pineal apparatus is something of a mystery and even figures in the mysticism of eastern cults. Called an "inward eye" and thought capable of being trained to receive otherwise unavailable information, the pineal body seems to have been a receptor and actor upon solar radiation at some former stage. There are cold-blooded animals today whose brains include a so-called "parietal eye" that is located beneath translucent skin and attached to a gland. This pineal gland is, or was, secretory in nature and vascular; that is, it was connected to the bloodstream for the purpose of disseminating its secretions. Some scientists believe that there is a connection between the reception of light by the functioning pineal eye and the dispersal of skin pigment. Scientists also think it possible that, even in man, there is some connection between the pineal apparatus and the reproductive system.

Another function of brains in lesser creatures like fish is the operation of the "lateral line" sensing mechanism. This little-understood network apparently receives signals from the environment. Most scientists believe the signals are due merely to the pressure of the water, but some think that they may be electrical or other such radiations. The lateral-line sense is nonexistent in higher organisms and even degenerates in some of the creatures who possess it at birth. For example, the lateral-line nerve system degenerates in frogs and toads during metamorphosis.

There are many other nerve connections that still operate in man, however. A dozen pairs of cranial nerves that connect the brain with all parts of the body and that take care of much of the running of the human machine have been identified. These twelve cranial nerves are as follows:

    I. Olfactory
    II. Optic
    III. Oculomotor (controls movements of the eyeball)
    IV. Trochlear (also controls eye muscles)
    V. Trigeminal (a tribranched nerve that controls eyes and jaw)
    VI. Abducens (another eye-muscle nerve)
    VII. Facial (controls facial and tongue muscles)
    VIII. Auditory
    IX. Glossopharyngeal (controls muscles of tongue and pharynx, or gullet)
    X. Vagus (controls heart and visceral muscles)
    XI. Spinal Accessory (a two-part nerve that controls neck muscles)
    XII. Hypoglossal (controls muscles at base of tongue)

An additional thirty-one pairs of nerves enter and exit from the spinal column, making up the autonomic nervous system, which controls the body at the unconscious level.

The Electrochemical Neurons   The old story that fish is brain food would seem to have some basis in fact. Fish were the first brainy creatures, and in fish, brain waves developed to fantastic electrical proportions. We know of fish today that have multiplied the primeval jellyfish's electrical capacity by hundreds of times. Some can generate a shock potential of six hundred volts. They are powerful electrical batteries, and some of this electricity resides, of course, in the brain. Man's brain is an electrochemical organ, too, but it produces only a tiny amount of power, about one-tenth of a volt at very low amperage. This electricity is conducted by the brain's nerve cells or neurons (shortened from the older term "neurones").

Having seen how the approximately ten billion nerve cells are grouped into specialized portions of the brain, we now turn to the cells themselves as more background for the mechanism of memory. In general, the cerebral cortex is structured in six layers of various kinds of cells—a surface layer of small "horizontal" cells; an underlying layer of "granulated" cells; a layer of "pyramidal" cells; another, more closely packed layer of "granulated" cells; another of pyramidal cells; and finally, at the sixth level, a layer of "spindlelike" cells. Furthermore, the number of

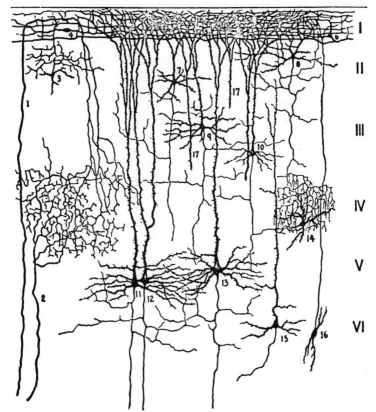

The general arrangement of layers of neurons in the cerebral cortex. From Lorente de Nó.

cells in the various layers varies in the different areas of the brain. The most slender nerve fibers are something like 1/25,-000th of an inch in diameter; the largest neurons are about 2/100ths of an inch in diameter.

Differing in a more fundamental way than the layers of cells are the three kinds of neurons found in the brain—sensory, motor, and internuncial or associative neurons. Sensory neurons enter the brain from the various receptor cells. The eyes have millions of visual receptors; the ears have many receptor cells that are stimulated by sound. Other receptors record pain, temperature, and touch. Motor neurons run the reverse circuit—from brain to muscles. Although there are millions of sensory and motor neurons, the associative neurons compose the bulk of the ten billion brain cells.

Obviously, some nerve cells are of great length in order to reach from the fingertips or toes all the way to the brain. They are of very different types, too; for example, a taste cell is far different from a Pacinian corpuscle, or touch receptor. Notwithstanding the miraculous makeup of these various nerve cells, they cannot compare with brain cells, the internuncial or association neurons of the cortex. It is this association area of the brain, this seat of memory and thought, with which we are most concerned.

Nerve cells have a vital difference from other living cells—they cannot divide. In fact, it has been suggested that this difference is necessary so that the brain will have fixed, stable communication pathways to and from receptors and effectors. From the time man acquires his maximum number of brain cells, he is never again so well off in the "mind hardware" department; at that point he begins to lose cells and continues to do so until his dying day. This loss of brain cells, for which we do not yet know how to compensate or substitute, is the reason for the onset in old age of loss of memory, reasoning ability, and interest. We become senile because we gradually lose our minds in the most literal sense—they just wither away, never to be replaced. Nerve cells, the most highly specialized of all cells, pay a great price for their differentiation—they are the most mortal of all cells. But while they live their accomplishments are marvelous.

Like other cells, the nerve cell consists of a nucleus surrounded by a mass of protoplasm. The nerve cell is distinguished, however, by "electrical terminals" not present in ordinary cells. Just as a man-made electric switch consists of input and output terminals, so does the nerve cell, or neuron. Most neurons have multiple inputs, or "dendrites," but only one output, called an "axon."

A neuron by itself would be useless because it is made to communicate, to send messages from one part of the body to another. Thus it is not surprising that neurons are found in intimate contact with each other. Each, or at least some, of the dendrites of a neuron are in contact with the axons or cell bodies of other neurons, and in turn these axons are in contact with the

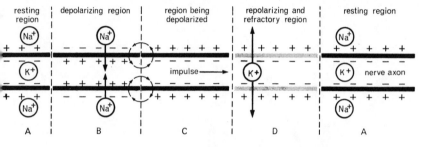

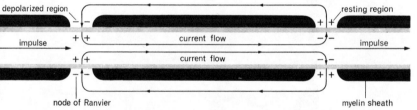

Input message from sensory organs to the brain is electrical in form and travels along neuronal axons. Initially, the membrane of these axons is positively charged on the outside (A). When axon is excited (B) membrane polarization is reversed. At the edge of the depolarized region local currents flow, spreading depolarization along the fiber (C). After the passage of an action potential, the membrane is repolarized (D).

dendrites of other neurons. These interconnections make clear the need for the huge area of the cerebral cortex, the gray matter of the brain. This large area yields a great number of interconnections for the multitude of neurons.

We have briefly discussed "action potentials" in the unicellular creature and in the nervous system. A similar electrochemical action builds up in the neuron in response to an input signal received through the dendrites. If the input signal exceeds a certain minimum or "threshold" level, the axon "fires" or produces a signal of its own that is passed on to dendrites next in line. The connection between dendrite and axon is called a *synapse,* from the Greek word meaning "to clasp." The scientist Charles Scott Sherrington coined the term since he saw from his

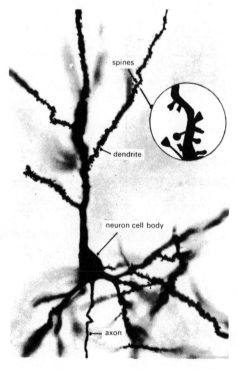

Detail of neuron in cortex as seen through a microscope. Dendritic "spines" are shown in circle.

studies that the two terminals seemed *to clasp* one another at this electrochemical junction. As we shall see later, the synapse is a far more subtle and sophisticated connection than anything electricians or electronics engineers have been able to build as they seek to duplicate the nerve networks nature has been producing for millions of years.

Like all cells, the neurons require sustenance in the form of oxygen and nutrients. A network of blood vessels almost rivaling the cortex in complexity feeds oxygen to the brain but protects it from poisoning by providing an intricate system of filters more effective than any other in the human body. The brain uses 25 percent of the total oxygen supply.

There are also neuroglial, or simply glial, cells that surround the neurons. These cells are generally thought to function as nourishers of the associative neurons. The name *glial* comes from the word *gluey,* because the cells stick to the neurons in clusters. This has led to jocular reference to "sticky state" memory, in contrast to the solid-state electronic memory of computers. As we shall see later, some physiologists believe the glial cells are far more than mere feeders of the neurons and are themselves a vital part of the memory process.

Memory   The evolution of the human brain is as intriguing as it is unexplained. Generally, it is thought that environment and natural selection provided the impetus for the brain to develop and improve. The erect walk of man, which freed his hands for the opposable thumb and for toolmaking, is often credited with evolutionary pressure. However, scientists have pointed out that there are a number of lesser animals that have the ability to walk erect and that have opposable thumbs but have not developed much of a brain. And some birds use thorns to catch insects, a toolmaking capability equal to that in monkeys and preman; yet the birds have not developed complex brains. On the other hand, the dolphin and porpoise, with none of the environmental advantages of man, have developed large and apparently powerful brains whose accomplishments probably include speech.

Alfred Russell Wallace was quoted earlier on his belief that the human brain put man beyond the vagaries of natural selection. Charles Darwin addressed himself to the specifics of that dominion:

> The mental powers in some early progenitor of man must have been more highly developed than in any existing ape, before even

the most imperfect form of speech could have come into use; but we may confidently believe that the continued use and advancement of this power would have reacted on the mind itself, by enabling and encouraging it to carry on long trains of thought. A complex train of thought can no more be carried on without the aid of words, whether spoken or silent, than a long calculation without the use of figures or algebra.

W. Tschernezky, of the zoology department of Queen Mary College, University of London, wrote in 1968 that he believes that vocal signalization and language were most powerful factors in the perfection of the brain. Furthermore, he stated that it was the brain itself that developed speech and language. Thus, in Tschernezky's view, it was intelligence that fostered evolution, not the reverse arrangement. This suggestion is only a repetition of Alfred Russell Wallace's comment referred to in Chapter Two.

Even in simple life forms the brain is a complicated organ. In man it is awesome in its complexity, so complex in fact that many leading scientists and philosophers believe that man will never fully comprehend his own mind because of certain inherent limitations. Nevertheless, scientists continue to probe for answers to the knotty problems of how the brain works. The knottiest of all is that of memory—how it functions and what is the basis for the buildup and retention of past events so that present and future action will have a basis for response. It should be remembered that the brain is an organ of survival and that memory is basically no more than a tool to aid in man's survival.

Chapter Four

LEARNING, REMEMBERING, AND FORGETTING

Memory is present to some degree in all living things—from the simplest organism to man. Memory is obviously the most developed in man, one of the factors that make us men and not lesser animals. Rather than merely react, we think, we reflect. To do this requires something to think about and something to reflect upon. That something is memory or, as purists among psychologists and physiologists suggest, the act of remembering. No one has seen a memory, the purists hold, even though all of us constantly perform the act of remembering, and everything we do stems from memory. It would seem wise to begin with a definition of the phenomenon, even though most of us are sure what it means.

Webster defines memory as follows:

> 1a. the power or process of reproducing or recalling what has been learned and retained esp. through associative mechanisms b. persistent modification of structure or behavior resulting from an organism's activity or experience c. the store of things learned and retained as evidenced by recall and recognition.

McGraw-Hill's *Encyclopedia of Science and Technology* says:

> Memory is evident in behavior when, after a passage of time without practice, past events are recalled or previously learned skills are performed.

Memory in the broad sense means both the remembered event and the ability to call it back into the mind. Webster's definition uses the term *persistent* and this term reminds us that memory is the persistence of an original event or experience. Before we can remember, we must perceive.

Perception Egon Brunswik, in *Perception and the Representative Design of Psychological Experiments,* makes this observation:

> Perception, then, emerges as that relatively primitive, partly autonomous, institutionalized, ratiomorphic subsystem of cognition which achieves prompt and richly detailed orientation habitually concerning the vitally relevant, mostly distal aspects of the environment on the basis of mutually vicarious, relatively restricted and stereotyped, insufficient evidence in uncertainty-geared interaction and compromise, seemingly following the highest probability for smallness of error at the expense of the highest frequency of precision.

There are simpler ways of putting it. Perception, according to *The New Yorker,* is "standing on the sidewalk, watching all the girls go by." Here is stimulus sufficient to provoke response, but as any parent knows, someone can be exposed to a stimulus without responding to it. A switched-on television set effectively muffles entreaties to youngsters that they wash for dinner. A cat stalking a mouse does not hear sounds it could not miss before the mouse appeared. Merely to see or hear is not enough; one must "attend" as well. The teacher raps on her desk in order to receive attention from her charges. The farmer who advocated love and kindness for the mule he sold added the provision that first the buyer must get the mule's attention by using a stick. Once we have attended, we are ready to perceive and to learn. Learning stems from attention, perception, and the resultant establishment of a memory.

Exceptions to the "rule of attention" exist, however. We learn a number of things without being consciously aware of them. How to balance a bicycle while manipulating turns is an example of a subconscious learning process; we memorize all the necessary swayings of the body and control movements of hands and feet but are sometimes unable to describe to another person just what is required. With subliminal advertising methods, products are hawked on ultrahigh-speed flashcards and not consciously seen; the advertisement is held to register in the mind as memory and is recalled when the consumer sees the product in the store.

Every perception becomes memory to some extent, but long-term persistence of all perceptions would lead to an overflowing storehouse. More seriously, recalling the needed memory at some future time would be difficult, if not impossible. An office worker may have just the information he needs somewhere in his office but may be unable to locate it in less than the time required to look it up again in the original source. The man with an overly cluttered mind is similarly handicapped. There is another principle, identified by psychologists as the principle of parsimony, involved in memory. *Parsimony* is defined as "economy in the use of a means to an end." The nature of memory is that it retains only what is needed. We are often convinced that memory is all too parsimonious in this regard, but usually the needed information is there if only we can dredge it up. Part of the parsimony principle is the temporary nature of a new memory or perception. Memory is usually fleeting, and unless we must make it permanent, most memories are not destined for this immortalization in the mind.

As you read this sentence, you will retain each letter or each word only until a phrase, a clause, or perhaps the entire sentence is complete and understood. In designing electronic computers for translation of foreign languages, engineers equip the machines with "lexical buffers" that have this sort of short-term memory. Because of grammatical and syntactical differences between languages, it is necessary to retain a number of words before attempting to translate from one language to another. Once the meaning is clear and the necessary changes are made from a literal, one-to-one translation, the lexical buffer "forgets" the collection of binary digits in its short-term memory even as you forget individual words almost as fast as you read them. However, even though each word is not remembered verbatim, the interested reader will retain the sense of what he reads.

Immediate Memory There is a psychological present that merges into what some writers have called "immediate memory" and that seems to last a few seconds, perhaps no more than ten or twelve. There is also a phenomenon by which we think we are remembering what are actually new experiences. This phenomenon is called *déjà-vu,* the familiar "I've been here before!" feeling. Immediate memory is the opposite side of the coin; we forget it almost as fast as we remember it. Arthur Koestler, in his book *The Act of Creation,* used an expressive term for this retention of perceptions—"mnemic afterglow." An analogous term is the "organic phosphoroscence" that Luys attributed to cells.

Immediate memory is easily tested, and this kind of testing is often used in psychological or psychiatric clinics. The average person can remember a series of only seven or eight numbers; when we request a phone number from the operator, we must often strain our memory to retain all the digits until we can dial them. There is salvation in the fact, however, that the brain uses tricks like remembering, for example, 602 as a single number. However, because direct phone dialing often results in many more digits, immediate memory must be reinforced with a scratch pad.

The insertion of a word with shock value into a sentence or speech might cause the word to become at least short-term memory. But for the most part the brain does not—perhaps cannot—truly memorize each and every word, even though authors and actors might wish this could be so.

Eidetic Memory Some people have what is commonly called a photographic memory; they can study a page of text for a short period of time and then apparently retain in their minds a visual image of the page. To demonstrate that this is true and literal imagery, they can read rows of numbers diagonally, backward, bottom to top, and so on. They can pick out the fourth name from the bottom of the right-hand column and the seventh from the top of the center column. The scientific term for photographic memory is eidetic memory. *Eidos* in Greek means "that which is seen," and an *eidolon* is an image in the mind; thus an eidetic memory is a visual retention of what has been seen.

Eidetic memory differs from the phenomenon of simply reconstructing something learned by rote. Most of us can say the alphabet rapidly and automatically, but this recitation is a serial-memory process in which A triggers B, which in turn calls up C. Asked to recite the alphabet in reverse, we take much more time

Youthful subject is timed as he inspects picture during tests of eidetic memory.

and perhaps even make a mistake or two. Experimenting further, we can commit to memory a page of numbers so that we may convince ourselves that we have a mental picture that is like a photograph of that page. But trying to call off the numbers diagonally or to pick out one number by physical location and not by reference to the others proves that we have again accomplished only serial memory. Eidetic memory seems to be different.

In seeking clues to the mechanism of eidetic memory, we may consider the visual "afterimage" that is fairly common. Staring at a pattern, particularly a brightly colored pattern or one with many contrasts, results in a temporary impression of that pattern on the retina. After the visual stimulus is removed, even with the eyes closed the pattern, reversed light for dark and in complementary colors, persists. Is this an eidetic or photographic memory? It does not seem to be, for the persistence time of the memory is short and fixed, whereas eidetic memory persists for a longer period of time. For another thing, the eidectic image is not color-reversed.

Eidetic memory is possessed by many young children, although it usually fades with puberty. Some scientists theorize that eidetic memory fades because with adulthood comes conceptual and symbolic thinking and remembering, whereas the child's mentality is more perceptual. As Koestler says, the child lives "in a world of images of great vividness, whereas the average adult's images are gray shadows."

Psychologist Ralph Haber has reported on a recent series of tests of the eidetic ability of more than five hundred school children. Haber notes that the results of more than two hundred tests of eidetic memory have been published, most of them prior to 1935. These earlier tests seemed to indicate that half the elementary-age children studied had eidetic capability, but in Haber's tests only twenty children were classed as eidetic.

Haber is convinced that eidetic memory is separate from normal memory and in fact even interferes with it. As little as five seconds of viewing produced the images. Duration of the eidetic image ranged from about one minute to as long as ten minutes in one subject. None of the children could prolong the image, although one girl reported that she could recall the image even after an intervening period of several weeks. A few children were tested periodically over a five-year period and aways produced eidetic images.

While the eidetic image is visual, it does not seem to be the same as a retinal "after-image" of the optical illusion type. During the tests, the children reported that they could move the images in relation to the background, although if they moved them too far they would "fall off." The retinal after-image is in effect burned into the receptors and cannot be moved about unless the eye itself moves.

The eidetic children were distributed fairly evenly over the second through sixth grades. Haber feels that the fact that he found no eidetic children in kindergarten or first grade was due to the verbal demands of the test rather than a lack of eidetic capability in very young children. There was no correlation between eidetic ability and sex, race, IQ, reading achievement, or personality.

Another memory phenomenon somewhat similar to after-images and eidetic or photographic memory is the "imprinting" phenomenon experienced by ducks. The first creature the duck-ling sees after birth is strongly imprinted in its memory and con-sidered ever afterward as its "parent." Psychologists who work with ducks have, in this manner, been adopted by them. Contro-versy exists concerning the significance of imprinting, and some psychologists categorize it as only an exaggerated case of normal phenomena. After all, they point out, imprinting isn't so very different from a baby's calling all males "Daddy."

Short-term Memory If a reader is impressed by a particular sentence in a book or story, he might want to memo-rize it—perhaps as a motto or in order to repeat to a friend as indication of presumption on the part of the author. To memo-rize the words, he will have to look at them again and again until he has learned them "by heart," as we persist in saying. A child who is sent to buy groceries often finds it necessary to keep his memory going in this fashion: "A loaf of bread, a can of peas, and half a pound of hot dogs. A loaf of bread, a can of peas, and half a pound of hot dogs. A loaf of bread. . . ." The mnemic afterglow is reinforced with each successive passage of the words through the mind.

Just as the computer uses the reverberating circuit or delay-line memory—or did in the early years of its development—so the brain may use such a circuit through a "neural loop" for its short-term memory. The learning process has, in effect, created a flow of current through a neural network. This current continues to circle, and as the network of neurons continues the reverbera-tion, energy is expended.

It is believed that this process of reverberation or trace formation may continue for more than an hour. This belief is based on tests with animal and human subjects in which various shocks have been administered at certain times following the learning of new material. Electroshock is one form of interference; drugs are another. Given soon after learning, such interference seems to erase the memory; when the shock is given later than an hour following learning, however, there is much less loss of memory. The longer the delay, the less memory loss. Interestingly, this shock treatment seems to have no effect on long-term memory; rather, it erases or diminishes only new memories.

Long-term Memory   Not all perceptions are doomed to die shortly after they impinge on the brain. A few survive the gradual fading of short-term memory to become long-term memories. After enough drilling and rote learning as young children, we committed to memory the alphabet, our address and phone number, and many other useful bits of information. Despite romantic concepts of enchanted looms of mental activity in a dynamic memory store, there can hardly be reverberating circuits for all our many and overlapping memories. Along with the principle of parsimony of memory commitment, there is probably also a parsimony of effort in storage; however, certain things do become *ingrained* in memory—an appropriate expression for the belief that there are established traces in the brain wherein long-term memory resides.

In a later chapter we shall consider how such traces, engrams, patterns, or whatever they may be are preserved in the gray matter. For now we will simply accept that there is some sort of mechanism that does the job. We have moved beyond immediate memory and short-term memory to something closer to permanence. Most of us will remember until our death what our names are and when and where we were born. We "know" for sure our nationality and political affiliation. There is a humorous story about the accountant and the instructions he secretly perused each morning—"Debits on the left, credits on the right." Fortunately, most of us have no need for such clues to knowledge of this basic importance. The fact that we don't need such clues doesn't mean that we don't forget even long-term memories if we lose a need for them, but there is evidence that even though we forget, the memory trace is not completely gone. We can invert the old saw—many a memory is forgotten but not really gone. Dig deeply enough with drugs, psychiatry, electrical stimulation, fear, or some other strong prodding device, and there it is.

Detailed and accurate recollections of the most trivial past occurrences have been elicited with drugs and electrical stimulation. For example, a psychologist has described the case of a bricklayer who was able to remember decades later the individual bumps and hollows on a particular brick he had laid on a particular day. His description was subject to checking and proved to be correct. It is as though even the individual words and inflections of every bit of dialogue are retained in spite of what has been said here earlier.

There is a hierarchy among long-term memories, with greater retention of those we class as abstract-thinking principles, concepts, and so on. A criminal most likely has not forgotten the difference between good and evil, even though he may plead so. Mathematical processes such as addition, squaring, factoring, and so on are easily retained for long periods of time. Spinoza's statement that "the more intelligible a thing is, the more easily it is retained in the memory, and contrariwise, the less intelligible it is, the more easily we forget it" seems borne out by our experience with memory.

Tests show that although there is about 30 per cent loss of rote learning within forty-eight hours, there is practically no loss of comprehension-test material. In puzzle-solving, those who learn a principle retain the ability to solve the puzzle, and those who only memorize the solution don't retain this ability. In general, the more complex a memory, the more likely it is to be retained. Another general rule, subject to qualification on occasion, is that older memories are retained longer and that newer memories are the first to be lost in senility or upon accidental damage to the brain.

Memory of geometric figures tends to become more symmetrical; squares blend into circles; the letter C into a circle. Irregular rectangles become squares; the asymmetric blends into symmetry. The principle of parsimony is operating again. Interestingly, three-year-old children tend to round off corners of a square when copying it, although they make circles well. Is this an example of the brain's natural tendency to parsimony?

The Categories of Memory
The descriptives *short-term* and *long-term* do not exhaust the types of memory. Scientifically speaking, we have four categories of memory or remembering: "redintegration," "recognition," "recall," and "residual memory."

Redintegration involves the bringing back of a complex recollection, such as the events of a dinner party, a vacation trip, or a semester at school. Redintegration is often sought in patient analysis or in courtroom proceedings and may be obtained by the use of drugs, truth serums, and psychiatric suggestion.

Recognition occurs when the subject sees that a present situation is parallel to one in the past. A new acquaintance reminds us of an old friend—or enemy. A multiple-choice answer on a test is recognized as the answer given in the textbook. Or a song rings the memory bell, as the one that was played at a first prom, at a wedding, or on some other momentous occasion.

Recall involves the repetition of an acquired skill, such as operating a typewriter, playing a song on the piano, or reciting a poem from memory. A person with "total recall" is considered to have an excellent memory, and an objective test in which a student must recall rather than merely recognize information is a more difficult task.

Residual memory is the phenomenon of partial retention. A long period of disuse will seem to obliterate a skill or fact once learned, but an attempt at relearning the fact or skill will reveal that at least part of the memory still exists.

Learning
There is a point at which long-term memory becomes what we call learning, for we generally learn by committing information to memory. As with memory, there are a number of seemingly different kinds of learning—rote learning,

classical conditioning, operant conditioning, and conditioned reflexes, to mention a few. Herman Ebbinghaus, a German psychologist, became interested in the scientific measurement of memory, which up to his time had not been reliably measured. There are critics who maintain that Ebbinghaus himself was guilty of unscientific test procedures in that he used a single subject—himself. However, his work was important and has stood the critical test of time. What he did was to perform sufficient tests to establish valid curves of learning.

Students are learning French in a group mode of automated instruction. The teacher sequences the educational items presented to the students via closed-circuit TV system, and the students respond in French to questions about the pictures shown. The computer records and analyzes student responses.

To eliminate such factors as meaningfulness of material, personal interests, and motivation of the subject, Ebbinghaus created nonsense syllables of three letters, some twenty-three hundred syllables in all. Then he set out to learn lists of these nonsense syllables. Beginning in 1869, he continued his tests for many years and in 1885 published his findings in a book called *Memory, A Contribution to Experimental Psychology*. The book was a benchmark in the science of memory.

Ebbinghaus was able to plot a memory curve, which demonstrated rapid early learning with a gradual tapering off in improvement. He also formulated a forgetting curve, which is a reverse image of the memory curve; the curve drops quickly but some memory is retained for long periods of time. The psychologist proved this himself by memorizing the poem "Don Juan" when he was in his thirties and by subsequently relearning the poem twenty-two years later. The memory curve showed that he learned (or relearned) faster even though he could not consciously recall any of the poem. Although some critics say that Ebbinghaus made no allowance for the fact that he might have been a better learner in his fifties, the results nevertheless showed that the poem was retained in residual memory and was there when called on.

Researchers have continued to demonstrate the correctness of Ebbinghaus's findings. Recently psychologist Harold E. Burtt read his two-year-old son three selections from Sophocles. Six years later Burtt had his son relearn these selections plus three Greek pieces the boy had not heard before. It took 435 repetitions for Burtt's son to learn the new pieces and only 317 to learn those he had been exposed to long before in a tongue he still did not know. Obviously something registered in his memory.

A piece published in the English journal *Mind* the same year as Ebbinghaus's book was published said:

> May we hope to see the day when school registers will record that such and such a lad possesses 36 British Association units of memory-power or when we shall be able to calculate how long a mind of 17 "macauleys" will take to learn Book II of "Paradise Lost."

Fortunately for lads the world over, schools have better things for them to do than to memorize *Paradise Lost,* but "memory power" is indeed measured now by such standards as a "memory quotient."

While Ebbinghaus was memorizing his nonsense syllables, other men were studying different aspects of memory. Sir William Hamilton, a nineteenth-century Scot, was interested in metaphysics. He discovered that the mind could count only six or seven objects instantaneously. This he learned by throwing various quantities of marbles on the floor. In 1871 logician William Stanley Jevons of England substituted beans for marbles. He found that he never made a mistake if there were three or less beans in a toss. At five beans to a toss, he began to miss occasionally; and if there were ten beans in a group, he was wrong about half the time. At fifteen beans to a toss, he was wrong almost every time.

These men were measuring the ability to perceive things accurately. In 1887, just two years after Ebbinghaus published his

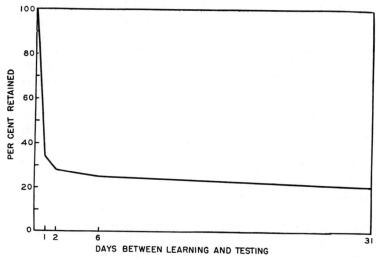

After H. Ebbinghaus.

Ebbinghaus's learning curve. A curve of forgetting is effectively the reverse of this one.

book on memory, Englishman Joseph Jacobs experimented with memorizing strings of digits. He found he could memorize seven or eight correctly at one reading. That we can memorize about as many items as we can perceive at a glance is probably not coincidence.

Fortunately for memory, an "item" can be much more than a single number or letter. One writer points this out with the number 149218627231416. This number has fifteen digits, about twice as many as the average human can grasp at one reading. However, if the number is broken down into 1492, the year of Columbus' voyage to the New World; 186,272, the speed of light in miles per second; and 3.1416, the ratio *pi*, the learning task becomes "as easy as *pi*."

Communication theory tells us that the information content of a symbol is the logarithm (to the base 2) of the number of symbols in the system. A binary digit, which is the kind of number a computer handles, carries only one bit of information because $\log 2 = 1$. Decimal numbers carry much more information because $\log 10 = 3.32$. The alphabet is even better because $\log 26 = 4.70$. Better still are words themselves, and a good estimate of yield per word of basic English is ten pieces of information. Experiments show that learning a list of words is about as easy as learning a list of digits. Thus the rancher who tallied his herd by counting the legs and dividing by four later improved his speed by noting that if he counted the horns and divided by two, the answer was the same. And he could count the whole cow—including all four legs, two horns and sundry other parts, much quicker.

Thousands of hours of learning tests have turned up some interesting facts. "Overlearning," a kind of supercharging of the memory cells, results in a slightly slower rate of forgetting. However, exhaustive drill in rote learning does not seem to improve the memory faculty generally. In fact, William James in 1890 took 131 minutes to memorize 158 lines. After thirty-eight days of practicing twenty minutes a day, he took 151.5 minutes to learn another 158 lines.

Another learning phenomenon is called the "reminiscence effect," which is evident in the student who, after a memorizing session, can read back twenty-five lines of a poem. The next day, with no further practice, he is amazed to find that he can recall twenty-eight lines. Another interesting phenomenon is the "Zegarnik effect," which suggests that better learning takes place if a task is not completed. The brain seems to retain better that which it has not yet solved or brought to full circle. Once the learning task is accomplished, the material fades more quickly from memory.

Thousands of tests have been performed since Ebbinghaus's time in efforts to measure learning. Much has been learned about learning, although it is perhaps impossible ever to know conclusively all there is to know about this process. In general the ability to memorize, or learn, is related to general intelligence,

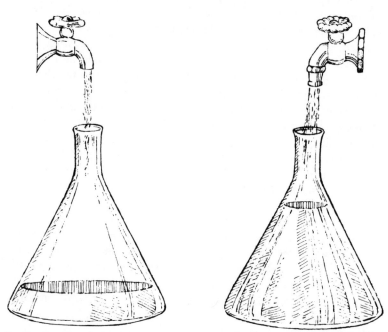

Beaker analogy indicates learning by level of water, forgetting by evaporation. As level rises, surface area decreases so that there is less evaporation. Fast input (right) represents easy material or quick learner; but in time the slow input (left) will fill the beaker just as high. Similarly, remembering appears to depend on the degree of learning.

and this fact was appreciated and put to use by Binet, the originator of scientific intelligence rating. Not all people learn at the same rate, but it is possible for the slow learner to learn as thoroughly as the fast learner.

There are different kinds of learning, of course. Pavlov's conditioned responses are low on the memory scale, and B. F. Skinner considers some simple learning no more than chains of conditioned reflexes. At the top of the scale are the cognitive concepts described by Karl Lashley, by the Gestalt psychologists, and by others.

Not surprisingly, most works on memory place the most emphasis on visual memories because the visual sense records most of our memories—or does it? Human beings communicate with speech; and radio, movies, and television have increasingly conditioned us to auditory perception. Are there parallels in the other sense modes for the visual memory phenomena that we have discussed? There seem to be, at least in the auditory. We immediately remember about as many items spoken as presented visually. And there have been rare individuals who seemed to possess eidetic ability with respect to sound. Beethoven, Mozart, and Wagner are said to have been capable of hearing in their "mind's ear" the full orchestration of a composition. One researcher reported that there are auditory eidetics who can hear a clock ticking after it has stopped.

There are other oddities connected with memory. Most of our memories seem to be in black and white. Dreams, for example, are seldom in technicolor unless the dreamer is deaf! And what of the ability called "absolute pitch"? Although most people, with the exception of those afflicted with color blindness, can recognize all the colors individually, it is a rare person who can identify a single note correctly. How do these anomalies tie in with memory?

Forgetting   Walter de la Mare set down in one of his poems these seemingly valid observations:

> Memory—that strange deceiver!
> Who can trust her? How believe her—
> While she hoards with equal care
> The poor and trivial, rich and rare;
> Yet flings away, as wantonly,
> Grave facts and loveliest fantasy?

Viewed from a scientific standpoint, however, memory is not arbitrarily untrustworthy, wanton, or capricious. Behind the hoarding and the flinging away lies a purpose, although that purpose is not so obvious as we might want it to be.

As Ebbinghaus showed, forgetting occurs with the passage of time. If we do not use a particular muscle, it gradually weakens, although with further use we can later rebuild the muscle. Colors slowly fade, and even mountains erode in time—for years these phenomena served as the basis for a common-sense theory of forgetting. The inability to remember an isolated fact is the most common form of forgetting. When we can link a memory to one or more traces in addition to its primary trace, the probability of recall rises proportionately. This linking process is similar to a cross-filing system. The customer whose name we can't recall instantly can be tracked down by street address, by referring to mutual business acquaintances, by consulting with clubs the customer might belong to, etc. The linking process also enters the picture when we meet a man who faintly resembles a pig, for example, and whose name happens to be Parker, which is similar to porker.

We are constantly reminded of the names of colleagues; we see familiar faces every day; two and two always equals four. But not often do we recall the square root of 7569 after having solved it once in an arithmetic test, nor do we remember the name and face of the bellhop who brought us a pitcher of ice water when we vacationed in San Francisco ten years ago. Some forgetting is to be expected, as we have discussed previously. Even when a faint trace of memory still remains, the process of relearning must often be undertaken before we are aware that the memory exists. John Locke seemed to put his finger on it when he spoke of the "gradual decay of ideas." More recently, however, psychologists have challenged this "decay theory" of forgetting.

Some, including Freud, believe that we sometimes simply refuse to remember. Their theory is that some memories are forgotten because they are painful or otherwise unpleasant. The act of forgetting can also be painful or unpleasant, as when we can't recall the name of an acquaintance or a customer's phone number that is literally on the tip of our tongue, or at least on the tip of our memory.

Some memory lapses seem perverse. We forget something we know as well as our name—sometimes it *is* our name that escapes us, although this occurrence is fortunately a rare one. When a recent memory or a memory that seems unforgettable is forgotten, the cause may be pathological. A bump on the head can wipe out a memory, temporarily or permanently. Sickness may have the same effect. Drugs, which can bring back buried memories, may also cause us to forget memories. The Greeks' nepenthe had that blessed property. Forgetfulness might also be caused by interference—attention to something else, absentmindedness, psychological stress (such as the knowledge that if we can't remember in ten seconds the name of the second president of the United States, we will lose a prize of $10,000 on a TV quiz show!), or other such interference.

In 1930 John McGeoch at the University of Iowa came up with the radical theory that there is no such thing as forgetting! According to McGeoch, failure to remember was actually only failure to remember the right thing; the forgetter has not done a proper searching job in the files of his memory. In the 1940s Arthur Melton of the University of Michigan evolved a theory that forgetting was really *unlearning*. Recent agreement comes from Sarnoff Mednick, who says that disuse does not cause forgetting: the best way to cause extinction of a conditioned response is to evoke it repeatedly in the absence of the unconditioned stimulus. Here is Pavlov's classical conditioning turned around, the unmemorizing of learned responses.

Today the interference theory is generally accepted by psychologists as an adequate explanation of forgetting. A librarian with a shelf of only ten books would have little difficulty in locating the proper one for a patron. When the collection grows to 100 the memory task is greater, and if there are 10,000 or 100,000 volumes, the retrieval of information will probably not be accurate and complete. One psychologist has suggested that the smarter, faster learner might also forget faster because he has more information in his mind and is thus subject to more interference. In apparent agreement, Sarnoff Mednick mentions that children recall a fantastic amount of detail because they have not had the wealth of experience that adults have had. Yet does this observation check with the notion that association helps to retain memory?

There are two kinds of interference—*proactive,* effective at the time of the memorization task, and *retroactive*. Proactive inter-ference encountered during the learning of information can include information learned earlier. Environmental distractions can be a factor, too, although recent studies by researchers at the London University Institute of Psychiatry seem to indicate that although learning is more difficult in a noisy environment, the information learned in this environment is retained better!

Retroactive interference includes later learning plus environ-mental distractions that occur during a critical period of some hours following learning. For this reason it is felt that the learning accomplished just prior to sleeping is most effective. One approach, called sleep teaching, actually claims to teach the sleeping or drowsy subject.

Psychologist William James's many experiments on learning included one involving alcohol. Prior to a speaking engagement, he imbibed so that he might forget his nervousness. He was most successful in that aim, but unfortunately along with his nervous-ness he forgot important parts of his speech.

In 1969 psychiatrists at Washington University School of Medicine conducted experiments on memory acquired when drugged or drunk and the later recall of such memory. This work stemmed from the earlier discovery that animals remembered better the training given them when they were drugged if they were similarly drugged when they were required to remember. In the Washington tests, forty-eight male volunteers were used. Some were given large amounts of liquor and then trained; in addition, control groups learned the same material. On retesting, the previously drunk group was sober, whereas the previously sober group was drunk. It was found that memory suffered when the subjects were in a different physical state when retested; the drunk group did worse when sober, and the sober learners did worse when drunk. Avoidance tasks, rote learning, and word association suffered most; recognition, as of a picture, seemed little affected.

Black Box   There is much for us to learn about memory from the phenomena of learning, remembering, and forgetting. Even though we are herein concerned only with the input and output of the black box of the memory, these outward manifestations should be clues to what goes on inside the mysterious brain. The physiologist, when he pauses from his work of dissection and probing with microelectrodes, is wise to spend some of his learning time peering over the psychologist's shoulder. Much of what we know of memory is necessarily inferred, and comparing the finished product with the raw material gives us some insight into the mechanisms operating within the factory.

Chapter Five

INTELLIGENCE AND MEMORY

Walter B. Pitkin is on record as having said the following:

> A rat runs himself ragged trying to get out of a trick cage. With one-tenth of the energy he thus squanders an ape will find how to get out of the same cage. And a man will succeed with one-tenth of the ape's efforts.

If this statement is true, a man would seem to possess a certain quality in a quantity a hundredfold that of the rat. That quality is generally called intelligence.

One psychology teacher reports having students hand in enough different definitions of intelligence to fill seven single-spaced typewritten pages. A distillation of these various assessments, however, produced the following succint statement: Intelligence is the ability to adjust to new and different situations.

The psychologist Thorndike expressed the definition of intelligence in more learned terms, which boil down to the same thing:

> Let c represent whatever anatomical or physiological fact corresponds to the possibility of forming one connection or association or bond between an idea or any part or aspect or feature thereof and a sequent idea or movement or any part or aspect or feature thereof. Then if individuals I, I_2, I_3, I_4, etc., differing in the number of c's which they possess but alike in other respects, are subjected to identical environments, the amount or degree of intellect which any one of them manifests, and the extent to which he manifests "higher" intellectual processes than the other individuals, will be closely proportional to the number of c's which he pos-

sesses. If we rank them by intelligence examination scores, the order will be that of the number of c's. If we rank the intellectual processes in a scale from lower, such as mere information, to higher, such as reasoning, the individuals who manifest the highest processes will have the largest number of c's.

This definition assigns a high place to memory as a factor in intelligence, for without memory there could be no adaptation to environment because adaptation implies learning. And learning is little more than memory. Despite all the jokes about absent-minded professors—one of whom was recently described as having made a tremendous scientific breakthrough, if only he could remember what it was—memory and intelligence correlate very well.

Our pursuit of the anatomy of memory encompasses some study of intelligence in the hope that an understanding of one phenomenon will lead to further knowledge of the other. Should intelligence be found to be inherited, for example, common sense would indicate that memory is likewise hereditary. The scientific approach to intelligence began less than a century ago, and Sir Francis Galton, a cousin of Charles Darwin, was among the first to address himself to the investigation of intelligence and to its measurement. He believed, and thought he proved, that intelligence is inborn. To improve the race he argued for "eugenics," the improvement of the breed by intermarriage of the most intelligent of its members. The reasoning behind this was Sir Francis's belief that ". . . in the process of transmission by inheritance, elements derived from the same ancestor are apt to appear in large groups." A later writer would satirically point out that "wooden legs are not inherited but wooden heads are." Ironically, Galton himself died childless and thus deprived the world of the continuing benefits of his own obvious intelligence.

Hereditary Genius   Francis Galton was born the same year as Gregor Mendel, in 1822. Here is poetic coincidence, for each man in his own way did much to further the science of genetics. Mendel with his pea plants laid the basis for the theory of heredity. Galton blazed a parallel trail in his studies of intelligence, a characteristic which he thought was as hereditary as the colors and other physical attributes of Mendel's plants. Like many other trailblazers, his experiments lacked refinement, and his biographer, Karl Pearson, describes Galton's scientific methods as the "crude extemporizations of the first settler."

Galton's forebears were intelligent, productive people; they were long-lived too. In his book *Memories of My Life,* he says of his longevity:

> My mother died just short of ninety, my eldest brother at eighty-nine, two sisters as already mentioned, at ninety-three and ninety-seven respectively; my surviving brother is ninety-three and in good health. My own age is now only eighty-six but may possibly be prolonged another year or more. I find old age thus far to be a very happy time, on the condition of submitting frankly to its many limitations.

His grandmother Darwin lived to eighty-five. Galton, like his cousin Charles, inherited the family intelligence along with long life. Sir Francis was unquestionably a genius. He could read at age two and a half and wrote a letter when he was only three. At five he was reading "almost any English book," telling time, and doing multiplication. Although his scholastic record has been described as undistinguished, he later made his mark in many scientific fields. As a youth he studied medicine. Later he became a naturalist, geographer, astronomer, meteorologist, and anthropologist, as well as a pioneer in the field of heredity. Galton wrote 15 books and 220 papers. He was a Fellow of the Royal Society and received a gold medal from the Royal Geographical Society.

Galton was an explorer and sportsman, a capable yachtsman, and even a balloon pilot. He invented a "Telotype" for printing telegraphic messages and for controlling heavy machinery remotely. He initiated the use of fingerprints in crime detection. As an outgrowth of his work on heredity, Galton advocated the methods of eugenics (a term he coined) for improving the race. In this suggestion he was perhaps more enthusiastic than scientific, and it is doubtful whether this approach to producing

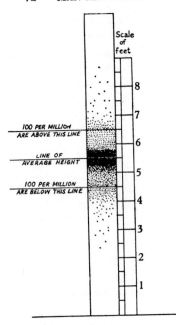

Scale of feet

8

7

100 PER MILLION
ARE ABOVE THIS LINE

6

LINE OF
AVERAGE HEIGHT

5

100 PER MILLION
ARE BELOW THIS LINE

4

3

2

1

Normal distribution of height in British population.

healthier and brighter people can ever be put into practice. However, he did make other more important contributions to the study of heredity, among them the suggestion for studying identical twins reared in different homes in order to determine the effects of environment.

In his book *Hereditary Genius* (still in print), Galton stated his thesis with refreshing candor:

> I have no patience with the hypothesis occasionally expressed, and often implied, especially in tales written to teach children to be good, that babies are born pretty much alike, and that the sole agencies in creating differences between boy and boy, and man and man, are steady applications and moral effort. It is in the most unqualified manner that I object to pretensions of natural equality. The experiences of the nursery, the school, the University, and of professional careers, are a chain of proof to the contrary. I acknowledge freely the great power of education and social influences in developing the active powers of the mind, just as I acknowledge the effect of use in developing the muscles of a

blacksmith's arm, and no further. Let the blacksmith labour as he will, he will find there are certain feats beyond his power. . . .

Citing published statistical studies of height, chest measurement, and other physical characteristics of the British and of other nationalities, Galton proceeded to make similar measurements of intelligence. He used the law of "deviation from the average" that M. Quetelet, the Belgian Astronomer-Royal, used in his scientific work. Just as the height of most people fell within close limits, so Galton found that most people also fell within the same mental range. A handful were well above this norm, and another handful were below, just as there were a few giants and a few dwarfs in any population.

Galton felt that these inherited mental powers were strictly limited and that no amount of study or education could extend them beyond certain levels. Just as one man might exercise his muscles with strenuous weightlifting yet never be as strong as another man who didn't even have to exercise, so a mediocre mind could never raise itself to the intelligence of a person born with superior intellect.

CLASSIFICATION OF MEN ACCORDING TO THEIR NATURAL GIFTS

Grades of natural ability, separated by equal intervals		Numbers of men comprised in the several grades of natural ability, whether in respect to their general powers, or to special aptitudes							
Below average	Above average	Proportionate, viz. one in	In each million of the same age	In total male population of the United Kingdom, say 15 millions, of the undermentioned ages:					
				20–30	30–40	40–50	50–60	60–70	70–80
a	A	4	256,791	641,000	495,000	391,000	268,000	171,000	77,000
b	B	6	161,279	409,000	312,000	246,000	168,000	107,000	48,000
c	C	16	63,563	161,000	123,000	97,000	66,000	42,000	19,000
d	D	64	15,696	39,800	30,300	23,900	16,400	10,400	4,700
e	E	413	2,423	6,100	4,700	3,700	2,520	1,600	729
f	F	4,300	233	590	450	355	243	155	70
g	G	79,000	14	35	27	21	15	9	4
x all grades below g	X all grades above G	1,000,000	1	3	2	2	2	—	—
On either side of average Total, both sides		500,000 1,000,000	1,268,000 2,536,000	964,000 1,928,000	761,000 1,522,000	521,000 1,042,000	332,000 664,000	149,000 298,000

The proportions of men living at different ages are calculated from the proportions that are true for England and Wales. (Census 1861, Appendix, p. 107.)

Example.—The class F contains 1 in every 4,300 men. In other words, there are 233 of that class in each million of men. The same is true of class f. In the whole United Kingdom there are 590 men of class F (and the same number of f) between the ages of 20 and 30; 450 between the ages of 30 and 40; and so on.

Galton's findings on intelligence among the British.

In each million humans Galton found about 250 of greatly superior intellect and 280 "true idiots and imbeciles." He qualified this figure slightly:

> No doubt a certain proportion of them (idiots and imbeciles) are idiotic owing to some fortuitous cause, which may interfere with the working of a naturally good brain, just as a bit of dirt may cause a first-rate chronometer to keep worse time than an ordinary watch. But I presume, from the usual smallness of head and absence of disease among these persons, that the proportion of accidental idiots cannot be very large.

Galton estimated that the brightest dog was smarter than the dullest human being! He also believed that the genius was as much smarter than the average man as the average man was smarter than the idiot or imbecile.

Nature Versus Nurture   A number of studies seem to corroborate Galton's theory of inherited intelligence. There are several classical families cited as proof, including the Jukeses, the Edwardses, and the Kallikaks.

Max Jukes was born in 1720, and 1258 of his descendants have been studied. Jukes sired a long line of feebleminded people, paupers, murderers, prostitutes, thieves, and criminals. By 1877 only twenty had learned a trade, and later records were almost as bad.

Jonathan Edwards, an exemplary "clean gene" type, was born in 1703. He married a superior-type woman, and 1394 descendants of this couple produced 133 college presidents, 65 professors, 295 college graduates, 100 ministers, 100 lawyers, 80 public officials, 75 military officers, 60 physicians, 60 noted authors, 30 judges, 3 congressmen, 2 U.S. senators, and 1 U.S. vice-president, plus many successful businessmen. Only Aaron Burr and Pierrepont Edwards, an unscrupulous lawyer, were considered black sheep.

Further evidence toward inherited intelligence came from studies of the Kallikaks, a case history of a "good" father mated with "bad" and "good" mothers in turn. Martin Kallikak had a son by a feebleminded girl, then later had more children by a girl of "good" stock. Two kinds of descendants resulted. Of 480 from the feebleminded mother, 36 were illegitimate and 33 became prostitutes. There were 143 rated as feebleminded, 24 alcoholics, and a variety of other defectives. Of the hundreds from the bright mother, only five descendants were not normal. Among the rest were many judges, doctors, lawyers, and other professionals.

There is a tendency to underrate and even to poke fun at these old studies as unscientific. However, more recent investigations carried out under careful conditions bear out the early findings. In 1922 Professor Lewis Terman began a long study of about

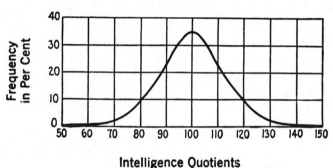

Intelligence Quotients

Normal distribution curve of intelligence.

thirteen hundred California youngsters with IQs higher than 140, and averaging about 150. The results paralleled the findings of the earlier studies of the Edwardses and the "good line" of the Kallikaks. The California geniuses were happier and healthier, and they prospered. They earned more money, won more honors, had fewer divorces, and their children averaged 127 in IQ, twenty-seven points above average, although not so high as the average of their parents. Here seemed proof of the correctness of Galton's thesis of eugenics.

Another proof advanced for inherited intelligence is the close correlation between height and intelligence. Between identical twins there is a correlation of .93 in height and .88 in intelligence. For fraternal twins the figures are .65 and .63; for siblings, .50 and .50; for parents and children, .30 and .31.

There is still argument over how "fixed" intelligence is. Will a person reach his potential on his own, or will shortcomings of nurture stunt his intellectual growth? Can a stimulating environment produce greater intelligence in a person? Implicit in both beliefs is the sure knowledge that even as silk purses don't come from sow's ears, neither can environment bring out something that isn't inherently present. Even those opposed to the idea of fixed intelligence admit that a person begins life with a certain amount of inherited intellectual capacity.

Maturation must occur before development can take place. In other words, a child of two is generally not yet able to tell time, in spite of any training he might receive. And rigorous training that accelerates the learning process beyond the normal pace does not seem to result in a brighter person years later. For example, children of preschool age can sometimes be taught such sophisticated subjects as geometry, but whether this training results in brighter adolescents and adults has not been established. IQ slowly increases up to about age fifteen when it stabilizes and later gradually declines.

Perhaps the most fruitful studies of the effect of environment on IQ are those of identical twins reared in different environments (Galton's suggestion). Rather extravagant claims have been made for increases in IQ of up to thirty or more points because of better environment; however, five to ten points is perhaps a more accurate estimate. And some psychologists feel that this estimate represents merely the development of the subject's innate capabilities. *General Psychology for College Students,* by Wendell W. Cruze, summarizes as follows:

> There is no evidence in any of the studies reported in this section which would lead the critical observer to believe it possible to change an idiot into a person of normal intelligence or a person of normal intelligence into a genius, either by the simple process of changing his environment or through the administration of glutamic acid or other drugs that may be purchased at the corner drug store.

Of course, a potential genius may fail to flower for lack of opportunity.

Today there is general agreement that intelligence is related to a person's genetic makeup, which is acquired by heredity, but that environment is a determining factor in how much of this inborn potential is exploited. Galton must receive credit for starting us on the road to recognition of this fact about intelligence. He also was among the first to analyze intelligence and to pin down the contributing factors that may be measured.

Chapter Four referred to the "macauley" as a unit of memory capacity. Baron Macauley, noted author and government figure, was wisely chosen, because anyone who can remember all of *Paradise Lost* is almost in a class apart—although William James also accomplished the Macaulean feat of memorizing Milton's epic. Galton cited Macauley for his fantastic memory, rating him a hundred times more intelligent than most men. He also mentioned Porson, the Greek, for his phenomenal powers of retention.

IQ Tests In 1883 Galton published his *Inquiries into Human Faculty and its Development*. This book has been called the beginning of scientific individual psychology and of mental tests. Not long afterward, the American psychologist J. McKeen Cattell devised mental tests that he gave to students at Columbia University. As had Galton, Cattell used his tests merely to study individual differences, rather than to put them to practical use in intelligence testing. Included in the Cattell tests was measurement of memory.

In 1904 the French psychologist Alfred Binet prepared tests of memory, attention, perception, and other mental abilities so that he could measure the intelligence of French school children. He collaborated with a physician named Theodore Simon, and in 1905 the Binet-Simon intelligence scale was developed. In 1916 the American psychologist Lewis M. Terman revised the Binet-Simon tests at Stanford University. Known as the Stanford-Binet intelligence test and revised in 1937 by Terman and M. A. Merrill, this test became a standard measurement of intelligence not only for children but for adults as well.

Intelligence testing branched out quickly from schools. In World War I, for example, Army Alpha and Army Beta tests

were given to inductees. Army General Classification Tests and
Navy General Classification Tests were taken by more than ten
million servicemen during World War II. Air Force "stanine"
(standard of nine) tests proved to be highly accurate predictors
of future success based on intelligence. However, despite these
results, the subject of intelligence testing to some extent remains
controversial.

OPERATIONS
    Evaluation
    Convergent production
    Divergent production
    Memory
    Cognition

PRODUCTS
    Units
    Classes
    Relations
    Systems
    Transformations
    Implications

CONTENTS
    Figural
    Symbolic
    Semantic
    Behavioral

"Structure of intellect" model proposed by Dr. J. P. Guilford, emeritus
professor of psychology at University of Southern California, shows the
numerous intellectual abilities.

One school of thought holds that a single test can fully
measure intelligence; another insists that there are a number of
kinds of intelligence. For instance, L. L. Thurstone suggested six
intelligence factors: number, verbal, space, word fluency, reasoning, and rote memory. However, these six factors are markedly
related, particularly in young children. England's Charles Spear-

man believed in two factors, a "g" or general factor involved in all intelligence and "s" or special factors related to particular problems. More recently, the American psychologist J. P. Guilford reported some eighty separate intellectual abilities, in addition to the theoretical probability of the existence of forty more! Despite criticism, the intelligence test presently represents the best index of an individual's potential ability.

The Prodigies Cardinal Newman said, "A great memory does not make a philosopher, any more than a dictionary can be called a grammar," and his point is well made. James Thurber complained that he had a memory remarkable only in the ability to remember the birthdays of all who had told him that date—Dorothy Parker, August 22; Lewis Gannett, October 3; Andy White, July 9; Mrs. White, September 17. Thurber said he got his extraordinary powers from his mother, who could remember the birthday of a girl James was in love with in the third grade in 1903.

Other famous people claim more useful memories. Arturo Toscanini memorized entire symphonies and conducted them without a score. Poor eyesight was his motivation. Politically motivated James Farley claimed he knew fifty thousand people by name! President Charles W. Eliot of Harvard knew the names of all his students.

Whether or not the abilities of mental giants depend principally on memory is open to question. However, it is interesting that many geniuses showed their abilities early in life and that these abilities seemed to be inborn rather than taught or learned. We shall begin with a few people who in later life made great names for themselves in the scientific world.

Ampere is famed as a mathematician and physicist, best known for his work with electrical theory. He invented the handy righthand rule for indicating the flow of current in a wire and also advanced a correct theory for magnetism. His biographers generally fail to mention that at age four he had taught himself mathematics from playing with pebbles and was able to carry out long, involved problems in his head. Carl Friedrich Gauss, a contemporary of Ampere and also a pioneer in electrical theory, amazed his father by correcting him in some payroll calculations at age three!

More recently, noted aerodynamicist Theodor von Karmann exhibited prodigious mathematical abilities as a child, multiplying in his head five-digit numbers until his father put a stop to this "circus trick." And Charles Proteus Steinmetz, the General Electric wizard, had a fantastic mathematical memory and could recall logarithms.

Although memory and intelligence are generally comparable and although many brilliant minds like Steinmetz, Ampere, Pascal, and others demonstrated amazing feats of mathematical and other memory, there are also well-documented cases of people of average mentality who possess fantastic memories. There are even the *idiots savants,* the learned idiots whose feats are difficult to comprehend. A knowledge of how their brains function at tasks matched only by the computer could shed light on the mystery of memory, but that knowledge is hard to obtain.

Oliver Wendell Holmes, no mental slouch himself, pronounced the following rather damning judgment on "calculating" prodigies:

> The power of dealing with numbers is a kind of "detached lever" arrangement, which may be put into a mighty poor watch. I suppose it is about as common as the power of moving ears voluntarily, which is a moderately rare endowment.

It is an interesting coincidence that Holmes used the watch analogy, for Galton did, too, although in the reverse context. Galton would undoubtedly have questioned that dealing with numbers should be equated with wiggling the ears. Let's look at some of the "lesser watches" into which the most amazing "detached levers" of mathematical memory seem to have been placed.

Memory and Mathematics   Thomas Fuller, a Negro born in 1710 and taken to Virginia as a slave, could do arithmetic mentally, including such feats as multiplying two nine-digit numbers together. He never learned to read or write and perhaps had to rely on the concrete numbers themselves rather than on symbols or conceptual shortcuts.

More publicized was Zerah Colburn, who was born in Vermont in 1812 and showed mental mathematical ability as early as age six. He toured America and then was taken when only eight years old to England, where he amazed mathematicians and scientists. Their amazement was undoubtedly tinged with envy, for young Colburn could give, *instantly,* the products of two four-digit numbers! Asked to raise 8 to the sixteenth power, he came up with 281,474,976,710,656 in a few seconds. Next he was asked for the tenth powers of the numbers 2 through 9 and gave them so rapidly that his listeners could not take them down and had to ask him to repeat his answers. He could easily extract square and cube roots of large numbers and even factor such numbers as 247,483. Asked to factor 36,083, he quickly replied that it was a prime number.

Naturally the audience attempted to find how Colburn's amazing eight-year-old calculator worked, and there were vague clues in his responses to the questioning. When the Duke of Gloucester asked him to multiply 21,734 by 543, Colburn said that he instead multiplied 65,202 by 181 but did not know why. Asked to square 4395, he hesitated momentarily and then came up with the correct answer, 19,395,025. He explained that his hesitation came because he hated to multiply four-digit numbers so he had to find another way to arrive at an answer; he multiplied 293 times 293, then multiplied that product twice by 15! In other words, he had mentally factored 4395, then performed the several multiplications—and all in a matter of seconds. Unfortunately, as he grew older and completed his education, his mental abilities in the mathematical field declined.

Although most prodigies seem to lose their abilities as they grow older, there are rare exceptions. George Parker Bidder was born in 1806 in England and taught himself to calculate by using marbles, buttons, and so on. At age seven he astonished his elders by correcting two of them who each thought he had the answer to an arithmetic problem. Bidder said they were both wrong and gave the correct answer. He was right, and there immediately began a quizzing that showed the youngster had fantastic powers.

At age eight he was taken about the country on exhibitions, and by the time he was twelve he was matched against Zerah Colburn, two years older than Bidder. Colburn's abilities were waning, and Bidder's were on the rise. Here are samples of the problems he was given:

A flea can hop 2 feet 3 inches a hop. How many hops will it take to go around the world if the circumference is 25,020 miles? And how long will the trip be if he hops 60 hops a minute? Answers of 58,713,600 hops and one year, 314 days, 13 hours, and 20 minutes were given quickly by Bidder.

A city is illuminated by 9999 lamps, each burning a pint of oil every four hours; how many gallons are consumed in 40 years? In 80 seconds Bidder said 109,489,050 gallons.

A heckler once asked how many bull's tails would be needed to reach the distance to the moon. Unruffled, Bidder replied that one would do it, if it was long enough.

The astronomer John Herschel posed a fairly difficult problem for Bidder. If light travels the distance from the sun to the earth in eight minutes and takes six years and four months to reach us from the nearest star, how far away is that star? Bidder calculated in his head the distance of 40,633,740,000,000 miles. So impressed was Herschel that he and a friend tried to get Bidder senior to put the boy in school at Cambridge.

Eventually he entered school at Edinburgh, completed his education as an engineer, and entered that profession. His mathematical ability increased during his life, and he must have been an asset to whomever he worked for. An example follows of Bidder's retention of his amazing memory until his death. As an old man he could calculate instantly the number of waves of red light (36,918 to the inch) that strike the eye per second. The answer was 444,433,651,200,000. Another remarkable fact about the Bidder story is that his two brothers had remarkable memories; one could quote Bible verses and historical dates, and the other was a mathematician and actuary. His son could visualize figures, and two of his son's daughters were similarly gifted.

Johann Martin Zacharias Dase was a German prodigy whose only ability lay in mathematics; he was otherwise classed as dull. But he performed the most complicated problems that have ever been done mentally. Until his time the record was the squaring of a thirty-nine-digit number; Dase multiplied two hundred-digit numbers. He also extracted the square root of a hundred-digit number; no other memory expert could do this for more than a fifty-three-digit number.

As we have seen, the average person can accurately count about six or eight objects instantly. Dase could accurately count groups up to about thirty in a single glance. In half a second he memorized twelve digits and their positions on the page so that he could instantly recall and locate them. This suggests eidetic memory ability. Like Bidder, Dase put his abilities to good use and spent his life calculating mathematical table values for *pi*, logarithms, and factors. Unfortunately, he died at age thirty-seven while in the middle of factoring the numbers from 7,000,-000 to 10,000,000.

There have been chess players who obviously had fantastic memories. Among these is Paul Charles Morphy, born in New Orleans in 1837. He was world-renowned and often played championship games blindfolded. It would seem to tax the memory to remember just the game at hand, but Morphy claimed he could recall every move of every one of the hundreds of games he played in championship matches! In fact, he later recorded about four hundred of these games, play by play.

How They Do It   Truman Henry Safford was asked to multiply the number 365,365,365,365,365,365, by itself. According to his questioner, young Truman "flew around the room like a top, pulled his pantaloons over the tops of his boots, bit his hands, rolled his eyes in their sockets, sometimes smiling and talking, and then seeming to be in agony, until in not more than a minute, he said, '133,491,850,208,566,925,016,658,299,941,583,-225'!"

The exclamation point is understandable; the rest of the performance is not. Other prodigies have described the agony of difficult calculations, the strain on their brains. Concentration comes in a number of ways. Some seem able to talk while calculating, even to profit by what might seem a distraction. A man named Jacques Inaudi, a shepherd who taught himself mathematical reasoning without even using pebbles, did not learn to read and write until late in his career; seeing a written problem actually made his work more difficult, as it did Bidder's.

Bidder was able to analyze his methods and freely told how he did his remarkable calculations. He said he used "concrete" numbers in his head, rather than the numerical symbols. This let him quickly divide a number like 984 into 24 groups of 41 each, he said. Interestingly, he did much better when the problems were given to him orally. In fact, to square a nine-digit number when someone read the number to him took him only one quarter the time it did when he had to read the number himself. Bidder explained how his mind worked:

> In mental arithmetic, you begin at the left-hand extremity and you conclude at the unit (right hand extremity), allowing only one fact to be impressed on the mind at a time (serial operation). You modify that fact every instant as the process goes on; but still the object is to have one fact and one fact only, stored away at one time. The last result in each operation, alone, is registered by the memory, all the previous results being consecutively obliterated until a total product is obtained.

Hearing explanations of how mental arithmetic is done leaves one with the feeling that here is a human computer prewired for instant answers to problems. For instance, Bidder described multiplying 89 by 73: "I multiply 80 by 70, 80 by 3, 9 by 70 and 9 by 3 . . . and the answer comes immediately to mind." Another prodigy said that when he was asked a question "the result immediately proceeded from my sensibility . . . I have often the sensation of somebody beside me whispering the right way to find the desired result."

More recent examples of mathematical memory experts are Professor A. C. Aitken of Edinburgh University and William Klein of the Mathematics Center in Amsterdam. Both have fantastic memories; Klein knows the logarithms of all numbers up to a hundred and of all prime numbers; Aitken once learned the value of *pi* to 802 places—in only fifteen minutes.

Klein calculated in only nine seconds the products of six pairs of three-digit numbers. In sixty-four seconds he multiplied 1,388,978,361 by 5,645,418,496 and got the correct answer of 7,841,364,129,733,165,056. When a dozen mathematicians at Manchester College attempted the same problem with pencil and paper, they took between six and sixteen minutes—and only one of them got the right answer! Klein works with audible numbers, muttering to himself as he computes; yet his brother Leo, who has almost as good a mathematical memory, remembers visually. If Klein makes a mistake, it is usually with two numbers that *sound* alike; his brother misses on those that *look* alike.

Professor Aitken mentally found the square root of 567— 23.81176180—in a few seconds. The more exact answer is 23.8117611996, but as Professor Aitken said, "It would be unreasonable to ask for anything more accurate." After attempting to describe how he performs his mathematical feats, he said, "Words cannot describe the speed of association in these matters, and the resources which the memory and the calculative faculty draw. The will rises and makes a most powerful imperative; brain and memory obey like an electric switch."

Without detracting anything from the diligent efforts of human calculators to improve their abilities, we must surmise that they began with minds hooked up differently from those of most of us.

Idiots Savants The so-called *idiots savants* are people who seem to possess fantastic mathematical memories and who are far duller than the experts already mentioned. Among such cases is that of twin brothers, each able to tell on what day a thousand years hence Christmas would fall.

Tredgold's Textbook on Mental Deficiencies documents some interesting cases. Among them is that of an epileptic idiot, age twenty-two, who could neither read nor write in spite of diligent efforts on the part of his teachers. He spoke only occasionally and briefly, yet "he had an extraordinary capacity for repeating fluently and with proper intonation everything said to him, whether in his mother tongue or in such languages as Greek, Japanese, Dutch, Spanish, etc." His case was said to be in the same category as that of imbeciles who are capable of reeling off cantos of poetry verbatim. These cases are reminiscent of the line from de la Mare's "Scholars": "Pollparrot memory unwinds her spool." The phenomenon is nothing but a rote replay of memory, of course. But oh to be able to explain such a mechanism!

In Tredgold's book the standout case of a calculating wizard is described as follows:

> A still more interesting case described by Lotte (1920) is that of a young man who was completely blind from ophthalmia neonatorium, but who developed the faculty of calculating to a degree little short of marvelous. For instance, he could give the square root of any number of four figures in an average of four seconds, and the cube root of any number of six figures in six seconds. When he was asked how many grains of corn there would be in any one of 64 boxes, with 1 in the first, 2 in the second, 4 in the third, 8 in the fourth, and so on [this is the problem mentioned in Chapter Three], he gave the answers for the fourteenth (8,192), for the eighteenth (131,072), and the twenty-fourth (8,388,608) instantaneously, and he gave the figures for the forty-eighth box (140,737,488,355,328) in six seconds. He also gave the total in all the 64 boxes correctly (18,446,744,073,709,551,615) in forty-five seconds.

It would seem there must be a certain memory pathway that is prewired for instant answers, because *idiots savants* can do little or nothing else in the way of performing an intelligent feat. Such rapid answers suggest something like a reflex arc rather than a conscious calculation.

Parallel Traits   Common sense tells us that intelligence demands good memory. Observation and testing bear out this intuitive judgment, and definition seems to equate the two abilities. Yet there is evidence that some who possess incredible memories are not highly intelligent and that some with prodigious memories are even subnormal in other aspects of mental power. In the latter cases, memory would seem to be innate, a wired-in ability. In some this ability so far transcends normal memory as to seem a freak, a mutation. If it were possible to trace the "circuitry" of the memory by dissection or probing with microelectrodes, researchers might learn much. Until such analysis is possible, we must be content to infer what goes on in the pathways of memory.

Unfortunately, the possession of exceptional memory does not necessarily guarantee genius or even normal intelligence to its possessor. But intelligence presupposes a good memory. And both of them, it is abundantly clear, are for the most part inherited and are only enhanced by environment.

Chapter Six

IMPROVING MEMORY

We typically joke about those things that are of great importance to us—money and sex are two obvious examples. There are countless jokes about memory, too. People tie strings around their fingers to remember, it is said, and ropes around their necks to forget. And there was the man who couldn't remember three things: names, faces, and—he forgot what the third was. His wife, however, had the worst memory in the world; she remembered everything.

Joking aside, everyone dreams of improving his memory for one reason or another. The politician is among those who profit from instant recognition of names and faces; waiters and other service and salespeople make more money in commissions and gratuities when they remember their customers by name. The struggling student prays for better memory as he crams for finals. And all of us who have arrived at the theater and have searched through empty pockets for tickets have wished for a better memory.

Semanticist Alfred Korzybski is known for stating that the map is not the thing. Neither is memory the experience, but Korzybski assigned it such importance that he dubbed it "time-binding." The poet "Woodbine Willie" put it more graciously:

> God gave His children memory
> That in life's garden there might be
> June roses in December.

Because of this need for better memory, much money is spent on courses of training, mnemonic devices, and other means for improving memory. There are countless books and articles on the subject. A current memory-improvement book contains a "selective" bibliography of nearly fifty other volumes on the subject. Many lecturers travel throughout the country and the world advising their audiences on how to cultivate a better memory. Memory seems certain to rank next to cleanliness in any list of desirable attributes, and the quest rivals that for the Fountain of Youth, perhaps because the two go hand in hand. The older we get the more trouble we have remembering, a fact that is hardly surprising because we are constantly losing those brain cells that store memories. What are the solutions offered at prices ranging from modest to expensive for a better retention of things we have learned?

Perhaps more important to our search for the mechanics of memory are the clues to be found in methods that seem to improve the remembering process. By carefully studying the input and output, can we infer what takes place inside the "black box" of memory?

Motivation for Remembering

Several decades ago Dr. Emile Coué offered his audiences and readers the very simplest of advice in the business of self-improvement. It is all a matter of motivation and desire, autosuggestionist Coué said. You are, or can be, what you think you are. And so Coué converts went through each day intoning the hopeful chant, "Every day, in every way, I am growing better and better." We could try this approach and simply will ourselves to do a better job of remembering, much like the youngster who remembers by repeating endlessly as he hurries next door to borrow the missing ingredients for a cake. Here the "circuit is kept reverberating," the memory process is retained as a dynamic thing and not allowed to fade. However, such a course might get in the way of other tasks for our minds.

Surely increased attention to the problem of memory will have a good effect unless it leads to worry over supposed deficiencies that in turn lead to further and real deficiencies. The number-two man aims to be number one by trying harder and probably benefits from this resolve. Resolving to do better, however, is not enough. Along with the will there must be a way, and many such paths to remembering are advertised. Along with the ten steps to bigger muscles or fourteen days to a more powerful vocabulary are similar tools for sale to build better memory. Most of these are association devices that put new facts to be remembered into compartments already labeled and categorized. If meaningful, these association devices can help, because approaching a problem from a number of angles seems to aid in its solution. If we can't recall the name of a member of our local club, we may remember that he is also our neighbor down the street or a member of our church.

There is a danger of reaching absurd extremes; for example, consider the case of the man who evolved a scheme for remembering which horses were black—they were taller than the white horses. And, unfortunately, we sometimes forget the memory device along with what we wanted to remember.

The Muscles of Memory   Body-building advertisements appeal to some of us when we read them in magazines; we would like to change from ninety-seven pound weaklings into muscular supermen capable of kicking sand into the faces of bullies. The secret here is the development of muscles by regular exercise. The weight lifter performs feats that most of us can only watch in envy because he has enlarged and strengthened his muscles by exerting them ever more strenuously. Will such an approach work with our brain cells? Can we strengthen our memories by wrestling with prodigious tasks of remembering, by forcing ourselves to remember by the hour? Unfortunately, memory cells are not amenable to this regimen.

We have noted that the psychologist William James tried this approach. First, he established his memory power by measuring the time it took him to learn a certain amount of material. Then he exercised his memory cells diligently and regularly, spending twenty minutes a day for thirty-eight days in rigorous memorizing. He then found that he was a slower learner than he had been before all his mental exercises! Others have tried, with similar negative results, this brute-force method of building memory.

Mental weaklings will probably never "beef up" memories the way weight lifters bulge their muscles; instead they must find better ways of processing the material they want to learn. An analogy would be for the ninety-seven pound weakling to learn karate chops along with using a masculine cologne to make himself attractive to the fair sex.

However, physical condition is not unimportant in memory. Certainly, if other things are equal, the more physically sound we are, the better our minds will operate. Good food, exercise, proper environment, and so on—all contribute to mental well-being. Illness takes its toll on mental powers just as it does on physical condition. However, this means only that we can assure operation of our memories at something near 100 percent of their capabilities through proper care of our physical bodies, not that we can supercharge our minds to an output of 200 percent or even 125 percent through hard work, vitamins, etc. Galton pointed out this limit to mental capacity a century ago.

The truth seems to be that we cannot really improve memory at all. Memory systems that work actually operate by making us learn better in the first place. The output of an electronic computer depends on the input; incorrect data, or data that is garbled or improperly coded, results in faulty answers when answers are requested from the machine. More pungently: "Garbage in, garbage out." The same is true of the human computer, the brain. Interference is the villain in most cases of bad memory. We don't forget, but the memory can become so clouded by other bits of information that we cannot recall thoughts as easily as we would like.

A Time to Learn   As we saw in an earlier chapter, learning is inhibited by interference encountered at the time of learning—proactive interference. Memory is also inhibited by retroactive inhibition, as has been demonstrated by scientific tests. Ideally, the mind should be resting after a learning period —material learned just before sleeping is generally retained better than material learned at other times. "Study before bed and perform on arising" seems a good and scientifically sound motto. Researchers John G. Jenkins and Karl M. Dallenbach found that only 9 percent of what was learned before noon could be recalled eight hours later. But when material was learned at bedtime, 56 percent was recalled after eight hours of sleep.

Hugo Gernsback, one of the fathers of science fiction, wrote a story in 1911 for a magazine called *Modern Electrics* about a man who learned in his sleep by listening to a recording. Huxley's *Brave New World* used a similar learning technique, called "hypnopedia." Youngsters sleeping in a state school dormitory were conditioned by pillow loudspeakers.

Since then there have been a variety of sleep-teaching experiments, ranging from nail-biting cures in a boys' summer camp to rehabilitation of prisoners in a California institution and the teaching of mechanical tasks during sleep, as well as general learning. Some success was reported in the "uplift" programs, with curbing of habits like nail-biting and drinking. Army researchers claimed success in training subjects to operate switches while asleep. However, sophisticated learning during deep sleep has not been demonstrated satisfactorily. Charles V. Simons and William H. Emmons did report that some learning seemed to be imparted by teaching subjects in the drowsy state preceding sleep. Sleep-teaching equipment ranged in 1969 from $149.50 to $395.

More effective, perhaps, are recordings pitched at the wakeful but lazy learner, although they are not so effective as this advertisement that appeared in the *New York Times Book Review* for March 30, 1969, would indicate:

> . . . Once a quiet voice begins to imprint new worlds of knowledge unobtrusively on your mind, over and over again until an indelible matrix of fact, philosophy and concept becomes etched in, to be used as a point of reference for the rest of your life. . . . Knowledge that lets you give answers while others are still trying to frame a question. All because you've converted your mind into a supercharged thrust of dynamic energy. Energy that absorbs information, stores it, causing the human mind to function as a kind of nature's sponge, making it recall, correlate, deduce with split-second timing and accuracy.

The Organization Mind   One strong theme runs through all the books and lectures on improving memory, and that theme is organization. This concept is not new; rather, it dates back to Descartes and even earlier. The French scientist-philosopher likened the mind to a room and pointed out that the mind could be neat or untidy. Obviously things can be found much more quickly in a well-ordered room, particularly if they are stored in a logical manner. In memorizing, then, it seems helpful to store facts neatly. Even more important is a cataloging system; and if we can make this system a crossfile, so much the better. Association plays a big part in memorization.

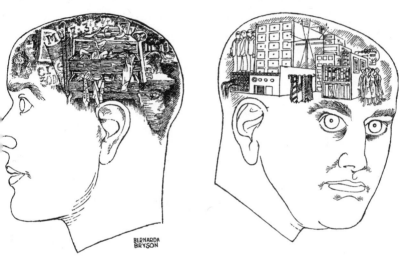

The untidy mind at left will have problems of memory. Descartes advocated the orderliness depicted at right.

In *Rules for the Direction of the Mind,* Descartes wrote these tips on organizing the process of learning:

> If I have first found out by separate mental operations what the relation is between the magnitudes A and B, then that between B and C, between C and D, and finally between D and E, that does not entail my seeing what the relation is between A and E, nor can the truths previously learned give me a precise knowledge of it unless I recall them all. To remedy this I would run them over from time to time, keeping the imagination moving continuously in such a way that while it is intuitively perceiving each fact

it simultaneously passes on to the next; and this I would do until I had learned to pass from the first to the last so quickly, that no stage in the process was left to the care of memory, but I seemed to have the whole in intuition before me at the same time. This method will relieve the memory, diminish the sluggishness of our thinking, and definitely enlarge our mental capacity.

A movie of many years ago, *The Thirty-Nine Steps,* featured a memory expert, William John Bottell, whose stage name was Datas. His description of his memory powers compares interestingly with Descartes's "rules":

> I am asked the date of the Great Fire of London. I give the correct answer, 1666, and immediately there arises before me a panoramic scene of that calamity, from its start in Pudding Lane to its finish in Pie Corner.
>
> When you are called upon to answer any questions, endeavor to call up some "mind pictures" for you will find their help of immense value. Remember that failure is the result of a weak mental impression due to lack of concentration on the subject matter you are endeavoring to commit to memory.
>
> One idea begets another; therefore, when memorizing one idea, kill two birds with one stone, and also memorize the corresponding idea. When you have ideas which are unconnected, you should establish an intermediary idea as a connecting link.

Memory Clues
The alphabet is learned by rote by practically all children, and it becomes deeply ingrained in memory. Repetition is a key factor here, but learning is aided by two other factors that may actually be more important than repetition itself. These are meter and rhyme. The ABCs are generally repeated in a singsong, regular rhythm, and there is rhyme: G, P, and Z. The *aaba* rhyme scheme involved is a basic one.

Electronic computers have an internal "clock pulse," to which regular beat all mathematical and logical operations conform. The pulse of meter seems to aid the human memory, and many a schoolboy has recalled a missing word because of the firmly entrenched rhythm of *di-dah di-dah di-dah di-dah* of iambic tetrameter, which means, in simpler English, that the accent falls on the second syllable and that there are four beats to the measure.

Rhyme is also an aid in memory, and the reciter at the school program or some other person attempting to recall a memorized fact is often assisted by the framework that tells him the needed word must rhyme with one already known:

> The stag at eve had drunk his fill
> Where danced the moon on Monan's rill.

Here are fifty-eight letters to be memorized. Organization first of all combines them into a much smaller collection of only fifteen words. These fifteen words are themselves grouped into two lines. Each line is made up of four beats, with the accent on the second of each two-syllable foot. And the last word in each line rhymes with the last word in the other. Grammar also helps the memory process by means of the subject, predicate, and modifiers—a doer, a thing done, and a qualifier of how done. Finally, the fifteen words are a group of words expressing a complete thought—a sentence. Obviously it is much easier to learn this couplet than to learn an unconnected string of fifty-eight digits or letters. Added to all the cues in poetry is the melody of song.

There are numerical clues for memory, also. The couplet quoted consists of two lines, line 1 and line 2. The religious Trinity is comprised of three beings, Father, Son, and Holy Ghost. There are Ten Commandments. The student studying for a test is wise to group his facts into numerical bundles. "I have four points to remember concerning why a certain war was lost," the student says to himself. "First of all . . ." Everyone knows the numbers one through four in order, and it seems to help considerably if numbers are tied to the points you have to remember. When the time comes for the student to recall information, he thinks, "First—Country X was limited in geographical area in relation to the size of the population; second . . ."

Another method of organization is to group information alphabetically. All words starting with *A* can be put in one group, all starting with *B* in the next, and so on. Alliteration, the use of successive words starting with the same letter, is masterful memory magic. Alliteration as a memory device is akin to the aids that poetry offers to memory.

Mnemonic Tricks An ancient tool for remembering is to group a list of items so that the first letters form a word. This idea is current in the acronyms that are used for governmental agencies and projects. United Nations Educational, Social, and Cultural Organization is a lengthy designation, but nobody has trouble wtih the mnemonic abbreviation UNESCO. There are some problems of course, in remembering whether NRA means National Recovery Act or National Rifle Association, but other clues can be developed to eliminate the problems.

There is another trick of making an easily memorized sentence from the first letters of a difficult list of words or names. A particularly appropriate one is the following short couplet:

> On Old Olympus' Tiny Top,
> A Finn And German Viewed Some Hops.

The first letters of these words stand for olfactory, optic, oculomotor, trochlear, trigeminal, abducens, facial, auditory, glossopharyngeal, vagus, spinal accessory, and hypoglossal, the cranial nerves we encountered in the third chapter.

Even spelling can be taught in this way. Students of an earlier day sometimes relied on the sentence "George Eliot's old grandmother ran a pig home yesterday" to remember the correct spelling of the much-used word *geography*. Geography students of a century ago were also aided by the visual cues of "Stokes' Mnemonical Globe," whose virtues were extolled as follows by its creator, William Stokes:

> An outline of the human face and head is seen upon the globe. Noting on what portion of the face or head the various geographical places are located, fixes their relative positions easily and indelibly upon the memory, and renders the study of geography not only interesting but fascinating. A child will, as an amusement, teach himself more geography in a couple of hours with this globe than the most indefatigable schoolmaster could thrash into him in a twelvemonth.

> With the Mnemonical Globe, beating a child will be found to

be of no service, as he will not object to take pains. Even adults, who have either never known much of geography, or who have let their geographical knowledge evaporate, will find that they can fix in memory the position of places upon the globe by this plan with remarkable ease and speed. Those who study the Mnemonical Globe will find that occasionally a little playful pleasantry with the geographical names will enliven the proceedings, and will produce and strengthen mental impressions.

Stokes's smiling globe was held to teach geography better than a beating would.

Among the "little playful pleasantries" were "mad rascal" for Madagascar, "you're up" for Europe, and "the bit" for Tibet.

Although such hilarity might seem to interfere with the memory processes, it was surely more pleasant than a thrashing!

Modern Memory Systems   More recently there have been developed what memory experts call topical systems for remembering. These are elaborations of the numerical and alphabetical systems that have been used for centuries, and they seem to have the power of the earlier systems in addition to new association values.

Topical systems use matrices of ten or more items to serve as anchors or pegs on which to put new things to be learned. One simple system given in *How to Develop an Exceptional Memory,* by Young and Gibson, uses the following "trip method." First, the student of memory commits to memory the following ten items:

1. Visualize the *entrance* to the terminal.
2. You are at the *ticket office* in the terminal.
3. Imagine yourself buying something at the *newsstand.*
4. Now you are in the *waiting room,* looking about.
5. Next, picture yourself going through the *gate* to the train or bus.
6. Now you are on board the *train* (or bus) [perhaps plane would appeal to some!] and finding a seat.
7. You are looking from the *window,* viewing a scene during the trip.
8. You have arrived at a *station* out in the country or in some other town.
9. Picture a *car* (or *cab*) in which you are to ride to your destination.
10. You have reached a *house* (or *hotel*) .

With this framework firm in his mind, the student is now ready to memorize a list of things to do. For example:

1. Buy some camera film.
2. Call a lawyer regarding a contract.
3. Buy a pair of shoes.
4. Look at some sweaters.
5. Meet a friend for lunch.
6. Take some children to the zoo.

7. Stop off at the optician's for some glasses.
8. Sign some checks at the office.
9. Wait for a long-distance call.
10. Go to a lecture on Switzerland.

The procedures are simply to put each of the items to be remembered into one of the topical boxes or matrix squares committed to memory previously. Here is how the association is accomplished:

1. Imagine yourself starting into the *terminal* with people stopping you so they can take pictures of you with their cameras, putting in *film* as fast as they can.
2. At the *ticket office,* the agent is showing you a *contract* and going over its clauses while people wait to buy tickets.
3. At the *newsstand,* all they are selling today is *shoes,* which are all over the counter.
4. In the *waiting room,* college cheerleaders in *sweaters* are calling on the crowd to sing and cheer.
5. At the *gate,* who stops you but your *friend* with whom you have the date for lunch.
6. In the *train* (or bus) you can hardly find a seat because they are all occupied by *animals,* from lions and tigers to monkeys and giraffes.
7. You are looking from the *window* and are studying the scene through your *glasses,* which show everything very clearly.
8. You have reached the *station* in the country and people are rushing up with *checks* for you to sign.
9. In the *car* (or cab) the driver hands you a *telephone* and says that he has a call for you.
10. At the *house* (or hotel) people are sliding down a snowy embankment, with mountains like those of *Switzerland* in the background and everyone in Alpine costume.

At first blush, this system is something like going around your elbow to get to your thumb, as the old-timers put it, or like counting the cows in a field by noting the number of legs and dividing by four. It would seem easier to make a list of the ten items and check them off. But the association system does work, and the ten-item matrix shown here is but a starter. With practice the number is increased to fifty and even a hundred, and becomes a very powerful memory tool indeed. You can shuffle a deck of cards and memorize their order in twenty minutes, for example. Just don't be as impractical as Thomas Dwight Weld, the memory expert from New England, whom Mark Twain described as a person who could remember a hundred new names and faces but who would walk out into the rain without his umbrella.

The Memory Experts Richard Rovere, writing in *The New Yorker,* commented on the abilities of memory expert Dr. Bruno Furst:

> So far as is known, a man's memory, like his intelligence, remains just about constant most of his life. Dr. Furst cannot increase the power of anyone's memory, but he can enable a person with a poor memory to make the best use of it. He cannot rebuild the motor, but by overhauling the ignition, adjusting the carburetor, and cleaning the sparkplugs, he can get more speed and mileage out of it.

Furst shrugs off Rovere's objections as semantics and insists that he *does* increase memory power. Much of Furst's approach agrees with the accepted scientific understanding of memory today. He stresses the importance of associations, quoting the laws of Similarity, Contrast, and Propinquity propounded by Aristotle and Aquinas. And he quotes Professor Robert E. Brennan, a psychologist, on the importance of concepts in memory improvement:

> Without the knowledge of general laws, memory must be burdened with ponderous items of information. The perfect mnemonic system is one in which phenomena are related as cause and effect. And because it is the function of philosophy to study such relationships, we can very largely supply the deficiencies of a poor memory by cultivating a philosophic turn of mind.

In his book *Stop Forgetting,* Furst lists three ways of memory improvement:

> Mechanical methods—deepening, prolonging, and repeating the impression

Intellectual methods—employing a logical, rational system and classification

Ingenious methods—artificial systems of memory improvement

Consider the following excerpt from Furst's book:

Just as a mason puts one stone upon another, connecting both by mortar when he is erecting a building, so must we connect every new idea with a familiar one if we want the new thought to stick in our mind. We are not always aware of this fact, but it is worthwhile to give it some thought.

You will immediately see the truth of this statement if you think of learning a foreign language. In order to learn that *light* is *lux* in Latin, we must form a connection between *light* and *lux*, and only if this connection or association is strong will it enable

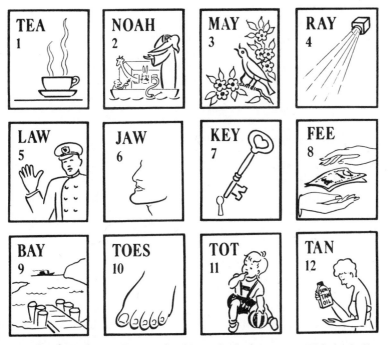

Sample of Dr. Bruno Furst's "hook" method of memory. This basic list is memorized and then used as a hook with which to associate new items to be remembered.

us to recall the foreign word whenever we need it. Once the pathway between *light* and *lux* is firmly established in our brain, we
will recall the one or the other without conscious effort, and even
without our will.

This analogy brings up some other questions however. Does
the connection Furst mentions between *light,* an English word,
and *lux,* a Latin word, need to be labeled English-to-Latin in
one direction and Latin-to-English in the other? And what about
the idea that a person must think in a foreign language to speak
it really well? Does this idea imply a complete foreign vocabulary? It would seem to.

When Furst discusses the best time of day for learning, his
theories do not jibe with those of scientific sleep researchers, as
we shall see in the next chapter. Furst says:

> Generally speaking, and admitting occasional exceptions, we
> may say that the evening sleeper (the type I first mentioned)
> learns and memorizes best in the morning. At that time his senses
> are at the height of their efficiency, and his brain cells are wide
> open for new impressions. The contrary, of course, holds true
> for the morning sleeper. He feels more or less drowsy during the
> morning hours and reaches the height of his capacity toward noon
> or even during the afternoon. Naturally, for him, the evening
> hours are the best time for learning difficult material. . . .

Furst goes on to say that learning a subject is no guarantee for
retaining such knowledge. In fact, he says it is entirely wrong to
assume such retention. A foreign language, he says, may be
learned "rather fluently" but lost if not used periodically. He
claims that the spacing of repetitive drill is even more important
than the repetition itself. For example, Ebbinghaus found that a
subject requiring 68 repetitions when learned at a single sitting
required only 38 repetitions when the learning task was spread
out over a three-day period. A more difficult learning task that
took 504 repetitions for one-day mastery was learned in only 342
repetitions over three days, with 158 repetitions the first day, 109
the second day, and only 75 on the final day of learning. This
was 30 percent less repetition. Going on this premise, Furst
recommends attempting only a "fair knowledge" of the material

at the first sitting and then refining learning during the practice periods that follow.

Furst classifies people as basically different types of rememberers. There are "eye-minded," "ear-minded," and "motor-minded" persons, depending on whether they remember best from seeing, hearing, or from making motions like writing or playing the piano. Although obviously none of us are all eye-

Stokes's mnemonical geography brought up to date. You can remember the four states in the United States that border one another by thinking of their first letters: U CAN.

minded or all motor-minded, Furst believes that these are innate qualities and that we will do best by primarily using our strongest memory tool. He is also an advocate of the "chain system" of memory, in which one memory recalls another, and so on. This system is in line with modern scientific theory that calls for sequential firing of associated circuits following the triggering of an initial recall.

Furst generally seems to advocate the muscle-memory analogy, but other writers on memory improvement speak strongly against this approach. Donald and Eleanor Laird are among these. In their book *Techniques for Efficient Remembering,* they point out a number of interesting scientific findings in memory work, including the following rules for learning that Herbert Woodrow used with a group of youngsters who had previously been tested on their memory ability:

1. Grouping and rhythm
2. Confidence
3. Visualization; seeing in the "mind's eye"
4. Trying hard to remember and recall
5. Memorizing by meaning rather than sound
6. Remembering the whole rather than parts at a time
7. Centering information in the attention
8. Association with things already learned

When the children applied this new knowledge of how to remember, they reportedly scored 36 percent better than in earlier tests on the same material.

The Lairds suggest that "I forgot" means that "I didn't try to remember," and they list the "Four R's of Remembering" as an aid to memory:

1. Register the experience so that it makes a trace in the nervous system.
2. Retain the trace.
3. Recall the experience by rearousing the appropriate trace.
4. Recognize the recalled experience.

The Lairds strongly support the association technique and advocate making a "diversity of connections at the start, including all the gateways through which you may want to revive the memory traces later."

Just as strongly they insist that no amount of memory muscle work can greatly "stretch" the memory. Recalling that Binet came across a memory expert who could remember forty-two numbers after hearing them once, the authors advise ordinary mortals to try to attempt only a digit or so improvement over the average number of digits that they can recall. Attempts to stretch the memory span from seven to ten may result instead in a reduction to five or six. A little stretching, say by one digit in the span, may come with practice. Real improvement, however, must stem from improved methods of learning and not from attempts to "lift memory by the bootstraps" through practice.

There should be instruction for the memory searcher in the Lairds' list of things we most forget:

> Names (of things as well as of people)
> Numbers and dates
> Unpleasant things
> What is learned barely enough to remember it
> Facts at odds with our beliefs and prejudices
> What we learn by cramming
> Our failures
> What we pick up incidentally without trying to remember it
> Things we think of only once or twice after remembering them
> Material we don't understand
> What we try to remember when embarrassed, frustrated, in poor
> health, or fatigued.

and things we least forget:

> Pleasant experiences
> What we review before going to bed
> Things that seem to us worth remembering
> What we give time to sink in before going further
> Things we talk about often
> Long or difficult material we stretch ourselves to learn
> Material we review, or think about often
> Facts and topics that interest us
> Our successes
> Material that makes sense to us
> Memories tied in with muscular skills
> What we use most frequently
> What we had a motive to remember for a long time when we were
> first learning it.

The Lairds advocate "overlearning" and agree with Furst and others on the desirability of learning in several sessions rather than in only one. They advocate a "three times" rule, stressing that one should be alert at each of the sessions and should rest when weary of learning.

In mentioning the "Zegarnik effect," the tendency to remember better the material involved in an unfinished task than in one that is completed, they point to results that are 50 percent better with unfinished tasks. This tendency can lead to strange side effects, however. Edison is described as being so involved with working out an invention pertaining to the telephone that he forgot his name as he stood in line at Newark City Hall to pay his taxes. So complete was this "retroactive" interference that he had to go to the end of the line while he wracked his brain!

Furst suggests "eye-learning," "ear-learning," and so on as methods better suited to different individuals, but the Lairds suggest that an individual use as many sense stimuli as possible to aid in learning. Lincoln read aloud as he studied, and Leo Tolstoi said he always thought and read aloud. In an extension of this double-stimuli technique, Dr. Wilse B. Webb of the U. S. Naval School of Aviation Medicine found that subjects learned equally well either reading or listening. But when they did both simultaneously, learning increased. Soldiers learning the military alphabet (A–Able, B–Baker, etc.) did from 25 percent to 40 percent better when they talked to themselves while memorizing.

Suppose that in addition to reading aloud, we simultaneously listen to the material and write it down? Then all three methods are reinforcing one another and being impressed on the memory from three different directions. About all we could add would be a musical accompaniment, along with smell and taste, to involve all the senses!

The other senses are involved in memory even though we don't realize it. Psychologists know that there are many "implicit responses" in the muscles—tiny muscle movements of the mouth and tongue as we read silently, for example, and muscle movements in the arm when subjects are asked to think about lifting a weight. One study, in which subjects held pencils between their teeth while learning new words, showed slower learning, apparently because they were not able to supplement the visual stimuli of seeing the words with the reinforcement of hearing them and saying them.

Motor learning is involved in many memory tasks, and may be recalled long after conventional recall attempts fail. A former printer tried unsuccessfully to remember where the various letters of type were stored forty years after he had done any typesetting. Only when he manually set type did the memory come back. This motor recall also works with a combination lock.

Eugenics, Euthenics, and Help for the Aged Memory Memory improvement, in the form of better remembering techniques, is aimed at the middle years of life. What can be done for the extremes—the newborn and the aged? Although work in this field is more controversial than in the field of remembering techniques and as yet has yielded dubious results, it is also more dramatic.

Francis Galton suggested eugenics as a means of improving the intelligence of mankind. Here is a possible approach to better memories for all. The children of geniuses rate considerably higher in IQ than the average of the population. Galton himself, as we have seen, demonstrated the irony of this approach by leaving no progeny. Governments are not yet ready to force the mating of compatible pairs in an effort to breed out dullards—or those with brilliant minds—and we may be thankful for that. Eugenics as a science is a dubious field and not nearly so clearcut an approach as Galton would have us believe. Some geniuses have dull children, and some dullards produce brilliant children. So love will doubtless proceed in its historically blind way—although perhaps it is not really blind at all.

Euthenics, or betterment of living conditions to improve people, is another approach, and one that would seem more likely to succeed in the improvement of man's physical and intellectual stature. Certainly, proper diet has enhanced the size and health of the race, and because mental power depends on health, it follows that minds are also healthier. *Mens sana in corpore sano.* Researchers have learned that some mental retardation stems from chemical deficiencies; when such deficiencies are corrected, the mind is improved.

Fish has traditionally, and perhaps with tongue in cheek, been held as "brain food." Now an experiment conducted by psychologists of the Institute of Child Psychology at the University of Groningen, The Netherlands, indicates that children who drank milk at breakfast were mentally sharper all day. As reported in *Sante Presse,* tests with eight hundred youngsters showed that those who had a glass of milk daily rated higher in mathematical reckoning, verbal comprehension, and precision and spontaneity of memory and had a greater capacity for comprehension and abstract reasoning than those who did not have milk.

The euthenics approach to better memory has even been attempted in South Africa during pregnancy. A decade ago Dr. Ockert Heyns, former professor of obstetrics and gynecology at

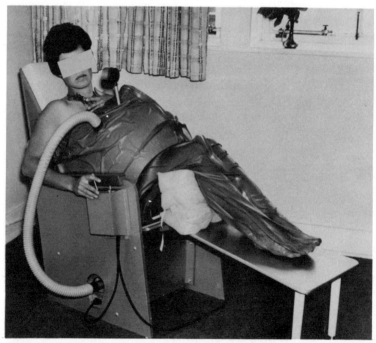

Abdominal decompression suit used by pregnant woman in experiment in South Africa. The technique is said to provide more oxygen to the fetus and guard against brain damage during pregnancy.

the University of the Witwatersrand, Johannesburg, suggested that decompression suits fitted to pregnant women should increase the amount of oxygen in the blood of the unborn child. Heyns's concern was with a condition known as anoxia, or hypoxia, in the fetus. This condition, in which a deficiency of oxygen affects the tissues of the unborn, generally occurs during the last three months of pregnancy. A lack of oxygen has seriously detrimental effects on the brain, and Heyns reasoned that neurons might be damaged or entirely destroyed in the last months before birth. Thus, providing additional oxygen should produce babies with relatively better brains.

Heyns made no claim for producing youngsters any brighter than their maximum genetic potential. He suggested only that guarding the developing brain against oxygen deficiency would

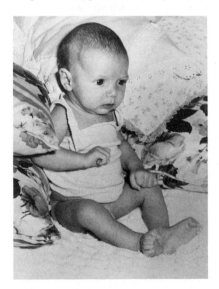

A "D", for decompression, baby, rated as brighter and more alert than normal.

guarantee intelligence closer to the genetic maximum. In particular, Heyns felt that imbeciles, spastics, epileptics, and other defectives could be avoided by the decompression technique. And he predicted that perhaps 40 percent of the decompression babies might prove mentally gifted. Heyns provided volunteers with the decompression therapy during the last three months of pregnancy, and tests of decompression babies seemed to bear out his prediction of an increase in the number of bright babies.

More recently a woman psychologist, Dr. Renée Liddicoat of the Council for Scientific and Industrial Research, has performed a series of controlled tests on 329 cases. Dr. Liddicoat tested the babies at one month, four months, and three years and found no significant difference in their intelligence than in the control babies who did not have the benefit of the decompression technique. She believes that Dr. Heyns's patients, being volunteers, represented brighter mothers and that their offspring could be expected to be brighter, on the average, than the offspring of mothers who did not request decompression.

Although the Liddicoat research has touched off a controversy, and it may be some time before conclusive results are available, it would seem that the idea is worth pursuing if only to guard against mental defects at birth.

The Aging Memory   A story is told of a group of old-timers sunning themselves in the park and discussing how old they were. One was so old he remembered when the cornerstone was laid for the first bank building in the town. Another was so old he remembered seeing Teddy Roosevelt when he was a Rough Rider. The last man topped them all by saying, "I'm so old I don't remember a damn thing!"

For this complaint there seems little that can be done, because it is a fact that thousands of brain cells die each day. Studies by Dr. Jeanne Gilbert indicate that people in their sixties recall 40 percent less of what they have just read than do people in their twenties. Experiments with various stimulants show that coffee, tea, and cola drinks seemed to help memory slightly. Pep pills in small doses may be somewhat beneficial, and for people who have a shortage of vitamin B, supplements of that vital substance help.

Dr. Holger Hydén in 1968 suggested at the third international conference on "The Future of the Brain Sciences," held in New York, that DNA with a "high intrinsic orderliness" be added to aging brains in an attempt to prevent the mental symptoms of aging.

Hydén uses the analogy of entropy in the nonliving world, the gradual increase in disorderliness or randomness. This phenomenon is the "running down" of the universe. Living systems manage to decrease their entropy, that is, to increase the orderliness of their cellular organization. With age this decrease in entropy reverses, with the natural result that the living thing dies or at least is noticeably degraded. Addition of fresh, ordered DNA, according to Hydén, might rejuvenate an aging brain.

Although he pointed out that the biologist has yet to produce an elixir of life, Hydén stated with some modesty that a successful counteracting of entropy in brain cells could, of course, change the whole structure of our society. Surely this is the understatement of the age. As we shall see in later chapters, there are developments taking place and discoveries being made by Hydén and others that suggest the possibility of startling changes in memory. One scientist involved in such developments has called the work "science fiction." Yet much of the scientific revolution taking place reads like the science fiction of yesterday.

Chapter Seven

SLEEP, DREAMS, AND MEMORY

In the song "Sweet Genevieve" the lyricist speaks more poetically than scientifically of the hands of memory weaving. In a similar anthropomorphic vein Shakespeare refers to "sleep that knits up the ravell'd sleeve of care." Miguel de Cervantes, in *Don Quixote,* had this to say of sleep:

> Blessings on him who invented sleep, the mantle that covers all human thoughts, the food that appeases hunger, the drink that quenches thirst, the fire that warms cold, the cold that moderates heat, and lastly, the general coin that purchases all things, the balance and weight that equals the shepherd with the king, and the simple with the wise.

Poets have the gift, and perhaps the duty, of assigning idealistic purposes to the aspects of life about which they write. Such a comforting and easy view cannot be shared by all who consider the strange phenomenon of sleep, the unconscious state in which most of us spend about a third of our lives. W. Grey Walter expresses the scientists' puzzlement over sleep:

> There is no clear explicit reason why the brain should need to spend a third of its life in repose. Is it for the sake of some other organs that the master centre closes down its receiving and transmitting channels? Is there some subtle chemical by-product of the brain's fierce sugar-furnace that accumulates in toxic quantities during sixteen hours of waking work? Or is our precious sleep but the genetic trace of the futility of nocturnal adventure in a wilderness of wide-eyed cats and jackals, an heirloom from remote

forebears who were perhaps better equipped for the fashioning of well-hidden nests than for the duel in the dark?

Walter suggests that as dawn creatures emerged from the "incubator sea" they were at the mercy of seasonal and diurnal weather changes:

> They must have suffered at noonday a delirium of over-action, and as night fell a sluggish torpor. Fortunate and fertile were those beasts who submitted with grace and discretion to the inevitable rhythm, curling away quietly in a private cranny as the impulses lagged in their cooling nerves.

Sleep is a fact of life, generally as accepted a fact as breathing or eating. But to the scientist it remains a mystery. Why does man—and why do the animals—spend about a third or more of their lives in the unconscious state? To give as a reason the fact that when it is dark there is not much we can do anyway is hardly satisfactory. That condition prevailed in the days of the caveman but no longer does. Furthermore, some authorities on sleep believe that the coincidence of sleep and the hours of darkness is a learned adjustment. An infant sleeps, at intervals, about eighteen hours of each twenty-four, with little regard for sun or dark. By age five the child has reduced this sleeping period to about twelve hours but it is still generally taken in several stints. This is called polyphasic sleep. Gradually we shift to monophasic sleep, and before age twenty the sleeper has reached the typical eight hours per day. This sleep is generally taken during the hours of darkness unless the subject works at night or has other reasons for going counter to conventional cultural patterns.

Man can adjust his sleep cycles to artificial clocks, as isolation experiments have shown. A study of Japanese children showed that they slept an average of one hour less per day than American youngsters of comparable ages. This is an indication of the adjustability of sleep patterns; nonetheless, all of us must sleep.

Nathaniel Kleitman, author of *Sleep and Wakefulness,* advanced an "evolutionary theory" of sleep. Polyphasic sleep, according to this theory, stems from a "wakefulness of necessity." The infant wakes at intervals because of hunger; the wild animal is awakened by danger. Monophasic sleep in adults among man and higher animals is "wakefulness of choice."

In sleep certain physiological changes occur. The heartbeat slows and the muscles generally relax. The stimulus threshold for sensory organs is raised—it takes louder sounds, more forceful touches, stronger smells, to rouse a sleeper. Deep body temperature falls slowly until a few hours before waking, when it begins to rise slowly again. Vision is the only sense that is naturally withheld during sleep. The eyelids close to shut out sight. The eyeballs diverge laterally, as would be expected with all extraocular muscles relaxed. But the iris muscle acts to constrict the pupil of the eye, an unexpected change since the normal reaction to dark would be for the pupils to open wide.

The "brain waves" change during sleep. Typically there is a shift from the alpha rhythm of wakefulness. These ten-cycle-per-second waves fade and the slower (up to five-cycles-per-second) delta waves take over. The delta waves are of greater magnitude, however. Research has disclosed localized "sleep centers" and "wakefulness centers" in the thalamus or hypothalamus or perhaps both. More recently, Michel Jouvet has found sleep centers in the pons, or midbrain.

Dreams   When we sleep we dream, and it is this aspect of sleep with which we are concerned here. Dreams stem from memory, but they differ from conscious thinking or reflection in that they seem random or irrational—an unconscious, uncontrolled, no-holds-barred turning over of memory. However, there are prohibitions and inhibitions, as Freud and others have pointed out. Dreams are useful tools for psychiatrists and psychologists, but they should also be helpful to the physiologist who is trying to find and understand the memory trace.

Early man most likely did not share the feelings expressed by Cervantes and others on the blessings of sleep, for sleep was understandably associated with death. As Gerard Manley Hopkins put it, "All life death does end and each day dies with sleep." Shakespeare forged a more forceful picture of this link:

> How wonderful is death
> Death and his brother Sleep.

Primitive man was terrified of dreams, too, and he sometimes believed that they were real and represented another life than that which he lived during the day. Swinburne's lines in "Atalanta in Calydon" reflect such a view:

> His life a watch or a vision
> between a sleep and a sleep.

Inevitably dreams became associated with, or even led to, superstitions. Dreams were associated with the nighttime wanderings of the soul, with ghosts. Dreams were visions, and some religions were founded on visions.

Interpretation of Pharaoh's dream. Woodcut by Stephen Arndes, 1494.

Early man thought his soul left his body and actually did all the fantastic things of which he dreamed. More scientific men reached the correct conclusion that dreams were not reality but were the workings of part of the brain while the conscious being slept. At the conscious level, the brain is activated and draws on memory to solve the problems faced in daily life. Of course, the unconscious mind draws on memory, too. Some dreams may be triggered, and surely are at least affected, by outside stimuli—a bell rings and is woven into the dream; a cold draft touches off dreams of being in snow country or in an icebox. But dreams spring primarily from within, and memory is their source.

As early as the second century, a Roman physician named Artimedorus published his *Oneirocritica* or *Critique of Dreams,* doing for dreams what a Kant would later do for pure reason. Artimedorus used the idea of symbology and interpreted dreams with a carefully devised code, which showed that dream symbols are mental puns that escape the "censors" in the cortex.

Dreams have been used—or misused—as gambling or betting tips, as predictions of the future, and as the subject of books. Indeed, books on dreams seem second in popularity only to those which tell how to get ahead by the power of personality. Dreams

Man Tormented by Dreams, 16th-century engraving after Raphael. Based on medieval belief that dreams were caused externally, by demons.

as extrasensory manifestations, such as predictions of the future, are outside the scope of this book and will not be investigated. However, interesting facts that may relate to the problem of how memory functions can be learned from dream research, because memory plays a part in the formation of dreams.

Scientific dream investigators date back at least to the early nineteenth century. A Scottish physician named Robert MacNish compiled reports to show that external stimuli caused or affected dreams—a hot poultice induced dreams of being scalped by Indians; wet bedclothes made the dreamer experience swimming nightmares; and heat applied to the feet conjured up dreams of leaping about on a volcano. The Frenchman Louis Ferdinand Alfred Maury, a contemporary of MacNish, was a little more scientific and actually had stimuli applied to himself and other sleepers. A hot iron held nearby made him dream that robbers were torturing their victims with hot coals. Water dripping on his head induced dreams of being in Italy in the summer and drinking wine to stay cool. Sounds made him dream, too, and he even added smells. Eau de cologne, for instance, brought dreams of adventures in Cairo.

Some of the first American dream research of a scientific nature was done by a woman, Mary Whiton Calkins, in 1892. She collected 375 dreams and classified them as to content and tone. Nine out of ten stemmed from events in the conscious lives of the dreamers; three-fourths were unpleasant. In the same era, Professor Will Monroe of the State Normal School at Westfield, Massachusetts, had female students in his psychology classes stare at colored squares before going to bed and then report their dreams in class next day. He learned that red was the most popular color in their dreams. Spices chewed before going to bed brought various dreams of cloves; however, one student reported that she dreamed the house was on fire—because the clove burned her mouth!

In 1923 the *British Journal of Psychology* reported on the work of researcher A. J. Cubberly. His approach was to paste "tensors" made of small pieces of gummed paper or dabs of glue on the skin or to use "detensors" of oil, butter, cream, or glycerine on the skin. These, he claimed, caused dreams that tied in with the particular area stimulated—dancing when tensors were stuck to the feet, sitting at a football game when one was applied to the backside.

The Interpretation of Dreams   There was—and still is—a school of dreams fittingly described as the "stomachache" theory. Although it is true that a surfeit of pickles and ice cream may result in protests in the dream department and that other physical aggravations at least color the dreams we have, an aching psyche seems to be the basic cause of our dreaming. Dreams seek to pluck from the memory Macbeth's rooted sorrow.

Sigmund Freud built his psychology to a large extent on dreams and their interpretation. Through the use of symbols, mostly sexual, he claimed to show that there was indeed a logic, however well hidden, in the process of dreaming. Dreams were catharses, the ridding of the mind of guilt feelings.

Freud published *The Interpretation of Dreams* in 1899. The Iroquois Indians, who lived in what is now New York State and Canada, antedated the Viennese psychologist by about three centuries, however. As pointed out in the April, 1958, *American Anthropologist* by Dr. Anthony Wallace of the Eastern Psychiatric Research Institute in Philadelphia, Freud and the Iroquois agreed on the following points:

> There are two parts to the mind, conscious and unconscious.
> The unconscious mind has desires unknown to or repressed by the conscious mind.
> Dreams are indicators of this repression.
> Dreams often are couched in mental "puns" whose double meanings do not offend the censor in the conscious mind.
> An interpreter of dreams is needed by the dreamer.

Wallace wrote that the two theories, Freudian and Iroquois, were no more divergent than Freudian and Jungian theories of psychoanalysis.

As recorded by the Jesuit priests who lived among the Iroquois of that time:

> In addition to the desires we generally have that are free, or least voluntary in us . . . (our souls) have other desires, which are, as it were, inborn or concealed. These, they say, come from the depths of the soul, not through any knowledge, but by means of a certain blind transporting of the soul to certain other objects. . . . Now they believe that our soul makes these natural desires known by means of dreams, which are its language. . . .

Standard dream symbols in the Freudian interpretation included the following:

Nakedness—A recapturing of the climate of Eden
Death of a loved one—Jealousy
Flying—Dreams of childhood: swinging, climbing, etc.
Falling—Temptation
Tests—Anxiety
Tooth-pulling—Sexual repression, castration
Swimming—A return to the security of the womb
Paralysis—Anxiety, inhibition
Robbers, ghosts—Memories of being awakened during the night as a child

In addition, Freud believed that dreams served to "protect sleep."

C. G. Jung became disenchanted with Freud's explanation of nearly all symbols as sexual and suggested that religion was really more pervasive in dreams than was sexuality. He also believed that each of us has an unconscious "race memory" that holds all the deep, emotional experiences of the race of mankind since inception.

Sigmund Freud, who pioneered psychological studies of dreams.

Jung believed in a "collective unconscious," a repository of all human experience from the beginning. As man's physical development is recorded genetically in the embryo and traces evolution from the fish on, so his mental and emotional evolution are imprinted in the collective unconscious and manifested in dreams. How else would man have retained the myths of life that existed prior to the written word? The difficulty, of course, lies in the fact that such myths are not verbalized but symbolized. Jung also thought the belief in flying saucers was a manifestation of the collective unconscious—ancient dream symbols connoting the sun god.

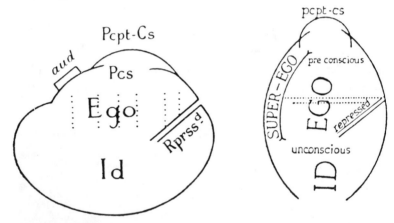

Freud's concept of the mind was more psychological than anatomical.

Thus Freud assigned to dreams the memory of base desires; Jung accorded them much nobler heritage. Erich Fromm has taken the compromise view that in dreams both these memories meet and work to resolve the problems besetting man in his day-to-day life. Today the interpretations of both Freud and Jung seem naïve and antiquated; researchers assign more meanings to dreams than religious symbolism and the repression of sex urges.

The Dream Watchers Ruth Krauss, in her charming book for little ones, *A Hole Is to Dig*, describes a dream as "to look at in the night and see things." Children with their faith would leave it at that, but scientists must dig even into dreams.

In the 1940s Calvin S. Hall, a professor of psychology at Western Reserve University, compiled case histories on about ten thousand dreams. Among his findings was evidence that people do not generally dream of earthshaking events like the dropping of an atomic bomb, or even of their own businesses or pleasures, but of more personal and emotional things. Most dreams reported were unpleasant (in contrast to mostly pleasant memories!), took place in familiar settings, and were peopled by family members or others with whom the dreamer was closely and emotionally involved. One-third of the dreamers reported seeing color in some dreams, although it did not seem to play any significant role. About half the dreams had erotic content, although Hall guessed that many erotic elements were not reported because of reticence on the part of the subjects.

Notable among the researchers of sleep and dreaming is Professor Nathaniel Kleitman, a physiologist at the University of Chicago. Kleitman had the thrill of discovering something that all previous observers seem to have missed: the fact that the eyes move in dreams as if watching the action. Kleitman stumbled onto this interesting fact while studying the sleep activity of new babies. One day in 1952 he noticed that even after a youngster went to sleep, his eyes continued to move under the lids. Curious, Kleitman began to study the electroencephalograph traces of sleeping subjects, and he found that there were frequent "REMs," as he called them, for Rapid Eye Movements. When he detected such wiggles on the trace of electrical activity in the brain, he went to the sleeper and shone a light in his face. The subject's eyes would be moving and, when awakened, the subject would verify that he had indeed been dreaming.

Involvement of the sensory neurons in dreaming had been suggested before Kleitman conducted his experiments. The American psychologist H. Trumbull Ladd, a contemporary of Freud, said that some dreaming was done by the retina of the eye. And Hermann Rohrschach, of inkblot fame, believed dreams were "kinesthetic," involving muscle movements.

Here was a most important discovery. The eyes generally move in perceiving things that are recorded in the memory; now it was established that in re-creating memories in a dream, or recalling memories to create a dream, the eyes likewise move. Why? Are these like the "implicit movements" of lips and other muscular areas when thought processes are going on?

In the journal *Science* of September 4, 1953, Kleitman described his findings. Twenty-seven times he aroused sleepers whose EEG traces had shown REMs. Twenty reported dreams. As a control check, he aroused twenty-three at a period of no REMs, and nineteen reported no dreams. Further research gave a total of 191 arousals, with 152 reporting dreams, an impressive ratio of 80 per cent correlation.

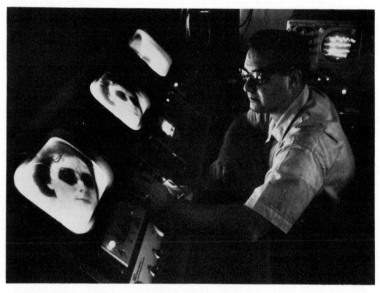

Scientist monitors sleeping subject.

Kleitman and his colleagues also found that dreams corresponded in length of time to the events dreamed about, destroying the old belief that dreams compressed great lengths of action into a few seconds. For instance, it had long been felt that the unconscious mind created a dream in a flash when stimulated by something external. Kleitman's research showed that this was not so. It was also established that in addition to the eye movements that accompanied dreams there were other muscle movements that corresponded to the walking, talking, and other activities undertaken in the dream.

It is believed that we dream only when the cortex is at a very low state of activity; that is, dreaming is done at the unconscious level and quickly forgotten. It has been proved that dreams fade quickly, that they are vivid immediately after awakening but that the details and finally even the structure fade away. Some researchers wonder that anyone ever remembers a dream at all.

Many people claim they never dream. Kleitman and other researchers doubt this claim, because all subjects tested did dream. In fact, it has been demonstrated that even strong drugs, such as meprobromate (a tranquilizer), and alcohol do not suppress dreams, although Benzedrine and Nembutal taken in large doses together eliminate the dream cycle. Conversely, experiments show that subjects cannot, through incentive or motivation, dream more than they would normally.

On the average we dream several dreams a night, but many people simply do not remember them because the conscious mind is not aware of them. The question comes to mind whether all dreams, as all memories at a conscious level have been proved to be, are remembered deep in the unconscious.

Threshold of Memory   Bruno Furst commented as follows on dreams and memory in his book *Stop Forgetting:*

> It is one of the strange phenomena of the human mind that memory continues to work even when the actual task of learning has ceased and even when we are asleep. It is the same peculiar occurrence which helps us to solve a problem while we are dreaming, especially a problem on which we focused our attention before going to sleep and which proved too tough for solution.
>
> The only explanation which is possible for both phenomena is the fact that our subconscious mind continues working and thinking while our conscious mind is asleep. The same mental power which produces dreams must be able to work on problems and to solve them. It is evidently wrong to think of our conscious and our subconscious functioning as two mental activities which are eternally divided. It is much better to think of them as two rooms whose separating wall is flexible and easily removable. It is

figuratively accurate to speak of the "threshold" between the conscious and the subconscious mind, for every thought can easily lapse from the conscious to the subconscious, and we are sometimes able to draw a thought from the subconscious over this threshold into the conscious mind.

There is growing evidence of more communication between conscious and unconscious memory than we ever dreamed of.

During World War I Austrian neurologist Otto Poetzl developed what is called a tachistoscope. *Tachistos* is Greek for "swiftest," and Poetzl's instrument was designed to present visual stimuli very briefly. A projector fitted with a shutter for showing a slide for only 1/100th of a second was used by Poetzl in studying aphasic patients, those who could not speak. The side effects

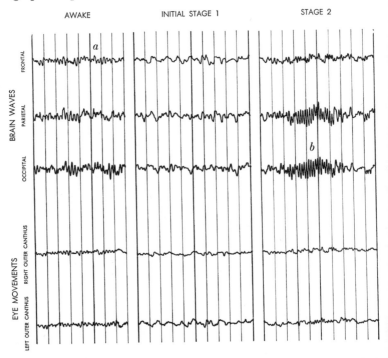

The various stages of sleep, shown by electroencephalograms compiled by Dr. William Dement. Waking alpha rhythm is shown at (*a*). Sleep

of the fast-action slides far exceeded the good Poetzl was able to do for his patients. Because the eye requires a little more than 1/100th of a second to take in a picture in order for the brain to perceive it consciously, patients could not remember the scenes Poetzl showed them in flash-card fashion. Yet strangely, they later recalled the entire scene—in dreams. This reaction was an indication that the perception was registering in the brain, not at the conscious level of memory but at the unconscious.

Poetzl seems to have been interested by the phenomenon, but he did nothing to develop it for a more practical purpose. Freud mentioned the tachistoscope briefly in a later edition of *The Interpretation of Dreams* but, poetically, the discovery of the real import of the tachistoscope took many years to dawn in research-

STAGE 3   STAGE 4   EMERGENT STAGE 1
                                              (DREAMING)

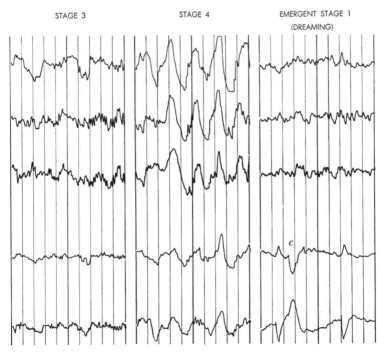

"spindles" appear at (*b*) during deep sleep. Waves are very slow and of great magnitude in Stage 4 sleep. Rapid eye movements are shown at (*c*).

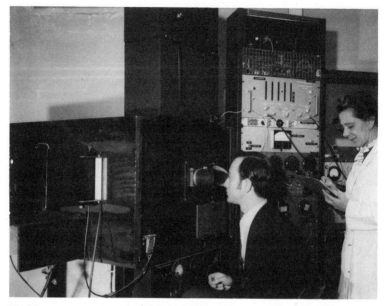

Tachistoscope permits viewing of material for very brief periods of time. These perceptions register on the unconscious and can be recalled later.

ers' minds. Not until 1954, more than thirty-five years after Poetzl developed the instrument, was the tachistoscope used again to any good purpose. In that year Charles Fisher, a psychoanalyst at Mount Sinai Hospital in New York City, flashed slides before hospital patients and rediscovered the delayed-action effect of perception. Subjects seemingly did not perceive what was on the slides but apparently recalled in dreams the material not available to the conscious memory. Excited by the results, Fisher tried the slides on himself. He had this to say about it:

> The subjective experience of tachistoscopic dreaming is very impressive. When one makes drawings of the dream scenes they seem to come out of the pencil, almost like automatic writing—the pencil draws by itself. Along with the automatic quality there is a compulsive need to put in or omit certain items.

Some writers saw the phenomenon as a "film negative with a latent image only developed in dreaming by the unconscious mind."

Fisher extended these tachistoscope experiments, which had previously been concerned mainly with repressions and unconscious wishes. However, in 1956 a Manhattan entrepreneur named James Vicary introduced "subliminal" advertising in a New Jersey movie theater and claimed that sales of the advertised products, Coke and popcorn, increased 18 per cent and 57 per cent, respectively, in the lobby! Despite many extravagant claims, however, subliminal ads do not seem to have become a way of life on Madison Avenue, perhaps because the subliminal ads on TV register when the customer is home in bed.

Why Do We Dream?

There are a number of theories on why we dream. Some researchers believe that dreaming is a type of temporary insanity; others feel that dreaming prevents insanity in the inactive mind by providing it with memories of sensory stimulation. Nathaniel Kleitman doesn't accept either of these ideas; he says that sleeping is a learned habit and serves no particular purpose. Most theorists disagree with him, however. John Keats penned some poetic thoughts on the function of sleep, and it begins to appear that he was on target scientifically as well:

> O magic sleep, O comfortable bird
> That broodest o'er the troubled sea of the mind
> Till it is hush'd and smooth!

For the bird of sleep does indeed seem capable of smoothing the mind's troubled sea.

In the chapter on learning and forgetting, we pointed out that memory seems dependent on one's "state"; for example, drunkenness and sedation represent different states than sobriety or alertness. Howard Shevrin and Lester Luborsky of the Menninger Foundation believe that the mind processes memories according to the rules of the particular state the mind is in at the time. The rules are different for dreams than for conscious memory.

There are differences in the way the brain calls on memory during dreams and during the waking hours. When awake, a person is capable of using logic, an Aristotelian approach to problems and solutions. In dreams, as we are well aware if we are able to recall them, the process proceeds instead by what one writer has called "drifting by its own emotional gravity." Others have likened dreams to the random workings of an electronic computer, programmed to roam willy-nilly instead of moving rigorously from Fact A to Fact B and hence to Result C. Dreams are often completely illogical—by Aristotelian standards, at any rate. The rules for dreaming are not the structured ones that we use in conscious thought. To be sure, dreams sometimes (though perhaps not as often as they are credited) solve problems seemingly insoluble by conventional approaches. And the process of "day dreaming" likewise produces some miraculous results.

In the next chapter we shall speak about Otto Loewi's Nobel Prize-winning discovery of the chemical transmission of nerve impulses. Loewi has recounted how he solved this physiological problem in a dream. He had first considered the possibility of chemical transmission in 1903 but had never been able to prove the theory. Then the solution came to him:

> The night before Easter Sunday of that year [1920] I awoke, turned on the light, and jotted down a few notes on a tiny slip of thin paper. Then I fell asleep again. It occurred to me at six o'clock in the morning that during the night I had written down something most important, but I was unable to decipher the scrawl. The next night at three o'clock, the idea returned. It was the design of an experiment to determine whether or not the hypothesis of chemical transmission that I had uttered seventeen years ago was correct. I got up immediately, went to the laboratory, and performed a simple experiment on a frog's heart according to the nocturnal design. . . . Its results became the foundation of the theory of chemical transmission of the nervous impulse.

Another case of dreams solving a scientific problem and leading to a great discovery is that of Friedrich August von Kekule, the German chemist. Born in 1829, Kekule became one of the leading lights in his field. He conceived the "Kekule structures" that were a pattern of the atomic arrangement in chemical molecules. His crowning feat was the visualization of the complex "ring" structure of benzene. This one he never did solve in his waking hours; it took not one dream but several over a long period to reach the sparkling insight. Here is Kekule's description of two of them:

> One fine summer evening I was returning by the last omnibus, outside as usual, through the deserted streets of the metropolis [London], which are at other times so full of life. I fell into a reverie, and lo! the atoms were gambolling before my eyes. Whenever, hitherto, these diminutive beings had appeared to me, they had always been in motion; but up to that time, I had never been able to discern the nature of their motion. Now, however, I saw how, frequently, two smaller atoms united to form a pair; how a larger one embraced two smaller ones; how still larger ones kept hold of three or even four of the smaller; whilst the whole kept whirling in a giddy dance. I saw how the larger ones formed a chain. . . . I spent part of the night putting on paper at least sketches of these dream forms.

This next episode was the final dream:

> I turned my chair to the fire and dozed. Again the atoms were gambolling before my eyes. This time the smaller groups kept modestly in the background. My mental eye, rendered more acute by repeated visions of this kind, could now distinguish larger structures, of manifold conformation; long rows, sometimes more closely fitting together; all twining and twisting in snakelike motion. But look! What was that? One of the snakes had seized hold of its own tail, and the form whirled mockingly before my eyes. As if by a flash of lightning I awoke. . . . Let us learn to dream, gentlemen.

Freud and his disciples used the patient's dream as a tool to probe his mind. Recently two psychoanalysts, Edward S. Tauber and Maurice R. Green of the William Alanson White Institute in New York City, have adopted a completely different approach. Believing that dreams are intuitive insights superior to "logical" conscious thought, the analysts use *their own* dreams as hunches to solve their patients' problems. They have compiled several case histories in an attempt to prove that this approach has produced good results. Tauber and Green wrote a book, *Pre-*

logical Experience, An Inquiry into Dreams and Other Creative Processes, whose title attributes other than logical bases to dreams.

Logical or not, dreams are being assigned greater importance on a number of scientific fronts. In a tongue-in-cheek letter to the British journal *New Scientist,* D. Herbison-Evans of the University of Sydney in New South Wales makes the following comment on memory and sleep:

> A number of the writers in your articles and letters about sleep and dreams failed to notice that out of all the senses only vision is switched off when we sleep. Now the human retina contains about 10^4 cells, each with a response time of about 10^{-1} second, so that in 10 hours it receives 10^{10} bits of information. It may be coincidence but the brain contains about 10^{10} cells. The obvious interpretation is that in sleep we are processing (and compressing) the day's visual information.
>
> It is interesting that a further 10 hours are required to process this information, before the brain is ready to accept some more. This implies that we scan through each bit 10^4 times before it is finally tucked away, and thus we relive the previous day 10^4 times in our dreams, each time at 10^4 times the rate of real time.
>
> It is also interesting that with our sense organ response time of about 10^{-1} second we live for about 10^9 seconds so that in our lifetime we effectively experience 10^{10} instants. Perhaps this is coincidence again but it does raise the possibility that we die when we do partly because we have run out of information processing and storage space.

At the 1969 meeting of the Association for the Psycophysiological Study of Sleep, researchers extended the concepts expressed by Tauber and Green and by Herbison-Evans. Dreams, the sleep scientists suggest, are manifestations of the mind reliving the experiences of the day in order to become better adapted to solving problems. Fittingly, the scientists used a bird to prove this theory.

Studies of chickens indicate that these creatures learn during their first day of life most of what they will ever know. Part of this learning is conscious, as in the imprinting phenomenon, but sleep is also believed to play a large role. During the first twenty-four hours the chick exhibits REM "dreaming" nearly all the time it is asleep. Following this cram course, chicks seldom exhibit the rapid eye movements that indicate purposeful dreaming.

Human babies spend half their sleeping time in REM dreaming, which some psychologists believe is an indication that they are learning at high speed in the early months and years. This is logical because there is everything to be learned. As knowledge increases with age, REM sleep shows a proportional decline to about 20 percent of sleeping time in adults.

In experiments with mice, scientists found that by depriving them of REM sleep, the mice forgot electroshock training that had been administered before sleeping. Analogous tests with humans seem to show that REM deprivation makes it difficult to adjust to stressful experiences. In sleep we seem to be conjuring up the events of the day and resolving our deep emotional problems in the process.

Sleep deprivation leads to hallucinations, susceptibility to brainwashing, and symptoms of gross mental illness. One subject, after remaining awake for more than two hundred hours, slept for more than thirteen hours—and dreamed 28 percent of the time rather than the normal 20 percent. Researchers interpret the onset of hallucinations and psychotic behavior that result from sleep and dream deprivation as attempts by the brain to dream while awake. As Wordsworth said, "The world is too much with us, late and soon," and the brain must escape periodically to digest the conscious experiences. In fact, in the two-hundred-hour sleep deprivation experiment, the subject's hallucinations were experienced at ninety-minute intervals and were most pronounced between midnight and 8:00 A.M., the time when the subject would normally have been dreaming.

The Sleeping Computer   Dr. Edmond Dewan, who earlier had performed experiments indicating that man can consciously control the alpha rhythm in his brain, is now interested in the sleep-memory problem. He believes that in sleep the brain is programming itself somewhat like a computer to function better in day-to-day problem solving. He says, "In higher organisms the

Dr. Louis Breger and Dr. Edmond Dewan observe sleeping chick during studies that show important correlation between sleep and learning.

brain is continually reorganized to meet the organism's current needs."

Dr. Louis Breger, of Langley Porter Neuropsychiatric Institute in San Francisco, has suggested that sleep is an ideal time for solving problems because of the individual's isolation from social constraints. Anxieties, he says, may prod the mind to search memory for similar problems stored there that may offer possible solutions. It is interesting that Webster defines "brood" as "to think anxiously upon." By this definition Keats's brooding bird was right on the mark.

Chapter Eight

PHYSIOLOGICAL THEORIES OF MEMORY

It is the belief of many that the brain is an organ that man will never be capable of understanding. Here is a paradox: we can understand anything—except the faculty that makes all else understandable. Some of our greatest minds, including Kurt Gödel and John Von Neumann, have pronounced this judgment. Indeed, the years have gone by since man first formed a relatively clear picture of the input and output of the brain, and no clear picture has emerged of how this phenomenon takes place; therefore, many psychologists have had to be content with the "black box" idea of treating only input and output.

It is comforting to argue as follows: what difference does it make how memory operates as long as we have it and know how to use it? The Impressionists founded a school of art based on final result rather than on structure—their paintings were images of impressions rather than faithful reproductions of reality. But always there are the atomists—or anatomists—who must dig beneath the surface to learn the structure and the mechanics of an event. In recent years a number of physiologists and others have begun to concentrate on what today's generation would term the "nitty gritty" of the gray matter. The brain—whether or not it can ever comprehend itself—is at least equipped with the germ of inquiry.

As long ago as 1953, scientist Ralph Gerard could write optimistically:

> Without memory the past would vanish; intelligence, often called the ability to learn by experience, would be absent, and life

would be "a tale told by an idiot, full of sound and fury, signify-ing nothing." Today the search for the fundamental mechanisms of memory in the nervous system is being pressed with hopeful enthusiasm. The smell of success is in the air and great develop-ments seem to wait just over the next ridge.

The memory seekers are still hopefully ridge-hopping. There are those who suspect that a pianist's memory is in his fingers and that the seat of reason might perhaps coincide with the physical seat, as in the aviator's ability to "fly by the seat of his pants." In a more scientific vein, some researchers seriously propose that memory lies partly in the spinal column, the retina, and even elsewhere in the body. A current text on memory says that the centrencephalic system "probably" plays an important role in gathering information for recording of memories. Integrated patterns are conveyed to the memory-association centers in the temporal cortices and, "by a mechanism as yet unknown," are recorded as memories. The exact site of memory, then, is hard to pin down.

If we are not even sure *where* memory resides, how can we solve the much more complicated problem of *how* memory functions? To a computer engineer, the innards of the machine are understandable; but a layman tearing open a computer would be completely baffled by any attempt to trace its workings. And man himself did not engineer his own brain, which is in-comprehensibly more complex than the electronic computer. Even the most brilliant and learned experts investigating mem-ory, as they study the brain through electron microscopes and watch the electrical activity on delicate instruments, are far from the certainty of understanding. In the face of such difficulties, much courage and even some foolhardiness are required of the researcher who attempts to blueprint the mechanism of memory. Fortunately, both these qualities are often possessed in sufficient quantities.

We have seen that the brain's motor area nerves form a picture—distorted drastically, but still a picture—of the body. Do memories similarly exist in the brain as tiny color slides or carbon copies of the actual occurrence? This is an obvious, if naïve, question. Some of us can recall memories with photographic intensity and clarity, and some even dream in color. We speak of the "mind's eye" and the simile is a good one, but no physiologist has yet uncovered a file of color slides upon opening up a patient's head any more than he has found an analogous repository of all the scents and odors the patient has smelled, the sounds he has heard, or the feelings he has experienced. In "Scholars," Walter de la Mare tells us that "poll-parrot Memory unwinds her spool." There are arguments in favor of such a spool. In the mid-1950s Wilder Penfield showed that an electrode stimulating certain areas of the brain evoked fine details of memory in patients, often memories from childhood. Such electrically re-created memories suggest the rerunning of an old movie or the replaying of an ancient tape-recording. Some psychologists have said that so much trivial detail is recalled that it hardly represents conscious memory at all. Every experience a person has ever had may be permanently stored in memory, awaiting only the proper trigger to evoke it. But we can be quite sure that memory's mechanism translates experiences into codes that bear no direct relationship to the actual happening. If we "saw" a memory trace face to face, we would not recognize it.

In addition to storing memories in his brain, man stores them in writing, in pictures, and on phonograph records and tapes. With microfilm he packs many bits of information into a tiny volume. These processes, and the more complicated feats of computer memory storage on tapes, discs, magnetic cores, and other elements, may be clues and hints of encouragement as to how the brain does the job of storing memories. But man has been guessing at the anatomy of memory for longer than he has had the computer for a model and thus has the advantage of a running start.

Disregarding the dualistic, "ghost in the machine" theory of animists and vitalists and assuming that mind is a function of body, we are left with several general theories of how we remember. One of these argues for "built-in memory."

The idea of the "memory trace" is an old one, hardly more than an updating of Plato's waxen impression. Sometimes it is called an engram, the term given it by Richard Semon in the late nineteenth century. Unless we continue to subscribe to the metaphysics of the animists, we must assign physical properties to memory; and the term "trace" is fitting. But the actual memory trace is not so simple as that term would suggest, not so definable as the pattern of magnetized material on tape or the groove in our latest hi-fi recording. For it is a trace like nothing in the artificial world, a trace with millions and perhaps billions of companions laid down in a repository that would just about fill both hands.

Prewired Memory   Aristotle's *tabula rasa,* or blank-slate mind with which we all begin, was unacceptable to many psychologists, including Immanuel Kant. Kant insisted that if the brain did not start out with much organization already accomplished, it could not hope to perform the tasks set before it. Asking that a random system of brain cells perform this well was like asking that all the card files in a large library be dumped helter-skelter on the floor and then be expected to rearrange themselves in proper order with no assistance from anyone.

There is much evidence to back up this "prewired" concept that Kant suggested. The existence of instincts and the ability of some animals to survive alone almost from the instant of birth argue strongly for a well-organized "memory" at the outset. The phenomenon of "imprinting" in baby ducks is a particularly good example. Here is an obviously well-ordered framework waiting only for the final, specific detail of the "parent" to be filled in. Once the duckling is imprinted, it follows the parent—even if the parent is actually a human researcher in animal psychology—from then on.

Although human beings are not so well organized at birth as the higher animals, their brains do develop automatically in early childhood. This is evident in Indian babies who are tied to a cradle board during the early years yet who learn to walk as early as those with freedom during this period. Many youngsters who are denied schooling at an early age nevertheless catch up several grades in a short period of time when they are finally afforded the opportunity to do so.

The fundamental purpose of memory, of course, is survival. The memory of past successes and, more importantly, past failures

Konrad Lorenz working with baby ducks during "imprinting" studies.

better prepares us to meet the challenges of the present. At one time an organism might respond directly and inevitably to light by moving either into or out of the light. Here is a reflex action, a direct and unchanging response to a stimulus. We can duplicate this simple system artificially, for example, with an electric eye to open the door at a supermarket. A single "neuron" will do the job—attach a dendrite to the photocell, an axon to the door-

Section of magnetic tape showing details of read/write channels. The three white channels are nonmagnetized tape areas. The four dark channels are magnetized. Two densities are shown: the darker is 556 bits per inch; the lighter, 278. Each lineup of magnetic particles is one bit.

opening mechanism. When the stimulus of breaking of the light beam registers on the neuron, it responds by actuating the door—now, an hour from now, and as long as people keep coming to the door and the power and mechanical parts last. We have a single neuron combining the afferent and efferent types, and this is all we need. This is not memory, however, but built-in reflex. And there comes a time in nature when simple response to a stimulus will not always be successful. That is the why the "associative" neuron, the net of such switches, and memory exist.

Suppose we add an "inhibitory" signal from a time clock to the circuitry of the automatic door. The door will now operate except during the hours when no business is wanted. This feat is

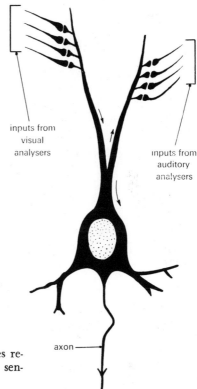

inputs from
visual
analysers

inputs from
auditory
analysers

axon

Diagram of neuron with dendrites receiving inputs from two kinds of sensors.

accomplished by making operation of the door mechanism depend not only on the switch in the photocell but also on an electrical circuit from the clock. Now the door opener checks when someone approaches to see whether or not it is the forbidden time period. Signals from the clock during off hours "inhibit" the "memory" of the system. The clock can be set so that the door will not open at all on Saturdays and Sundays.

A forerunner of this door opener would have caused the door

to open without fail each time the light beam was broken. Now, however, the mechanism searches its memory to make sure of its response. If the day is Saturday or Sunday, as established by a cue from the calendar, or if the time is lunch time any day, the response is negative—the door doesn't open. We might say that the mechanism has been taught—or that it remembers—not to open the door under certain conditions. We might also classify its circuits as excitatory and inhibitory.

Let's try a further analogy. We have not made a very secure mechanical setup, and the inhibiting neurons slip far enough so that they become inoperative. Then when a burglar approaches the door at midnight on Saturday or at noon on Sunday, the door pops open. We repair the inhibitors, making the connection tighter. Once more one slips free, but finally we tighten it so that it makes an indentation on the main neuron and therefore remains in place. Now we have a permanent memory system that will probably last until parts fail or the power dies.

Regardless of the fact that much information may already be wired into the brain in the form of genetic coding, instinct, reflex, racial memory, or whatever, it is even more obvious that each of us must add much new experiential information to memory if it is to serve us in adapting to environmental changes. We look now at the "memory trace," the record of acquired experience.

The Acquired Memory Trace   Plato, in "Theaetetus," has Socrates say:

> The soul is endowed with a bed of modeling wax whose thickness, consistency, and purity vary from one individual to another. Now this is the gift of the mother of Muses, Mnemosyne, for the wax receives the impression of the sensations and thoughts, which appear as impressions in relief similar to the marks of a signet. This imprint is like a mark of the thing, and affords a means of recalling it. A mark that disappears, or has not been properly imprinted, is forgotten by us.

Aristotle also conceived of memory as a lasting impression in the wax of the receptive brain. This "mark of the thing" approach has a common-sense appeal and has been accepted by many researchers since the ancient Greeks first put forth the idea. Descartes considered memories as "traces and vestiges that are just like the folds in a piece of paper that make it easier to fold it again." His disciple Nicolas Malebranche said: "Imagination is only the power the soul has of forming images of objects for itself, by imprinting them so to speak in the brain."

And by 1900, Paul Sollier could report general agreement that a sensation or perception produced as the result of stimulation of the cells of the cortex resulted in a permanent modification in the cortex that allowed the perception to be reproduced.

> Let us assume that a nervous cell has never functioned. When a stimulus comes to the end of its cylindrax, it begins to vibrate; under this influence a new molecular state tends to be produced: the cell becomes turgescent; and so on. But a second stimulus follows; this time the molecular cohesion is not so great as the first time, the disjunction takes place more easily. . . . If then, for some reason or other, this molecular state was reproduced, an observer who had seen it answer a given stimulus would be right in believing that it was this stimulus which was operating again. . . .

Although the basic idea of memory was still one of an impression in wax, the men pursuing the idea were more scientific and the particulars more sophisticated. The psychologist William McDougall, writing in 1911, agreed with Sollier:

> Looked at broadly from the biological standpoint the essential function of mental processes appears as the bringing of past experience to bear in the regulation of present behaviour. . . .
>
>   . . . the minute study in recent years of the processes of mental association and reproduction has shown that they obey laws which seem to be identical with those of the formation and operation of habits. Now, there is no room for doubt that the acquisition of a habit consists in the consolidation, improvement, or wearing smooth of such paths of communication between nerve cells, or, as it is commonly put, in the formation of paths of low resistance in the nervous system.

McDougall also touched on the complexity of the memory trace:

It is recognized that the physical correlate in the brain of the perception of a relatively simple object must run its course in a large number of neurons, and that the memory-image or representation of that object must also have for its physical correlate a very complex process distributed throughout a large number of the same neurons and, perhaps, through others also. The only conception that we can form of a memory-trace in the brain as a neural disposition, the continuance of which might be the condition of the possibility of representation, is, then, that of a number of neurons intimately linked together to form a functional system; and the linking together of the members of the system must be supposed to be brought about by the spread of the excitation process or current of nervous energy from member to member throughout the system at the moment of perception.

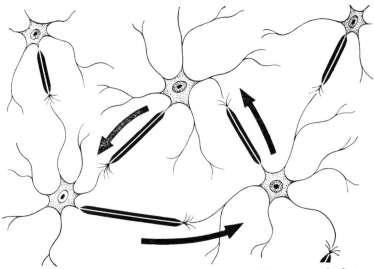

Early theory of memory formulated in the 1920s proposed that a memory was stored by changes in the connections between certain individual neurons, setting up a new and unique circuit. The simplest circuit possible connects three neurons in a triangle. Electrical brain patterns, mirrored in EEG traces, were thought to be the result of these reverberating circuits. The theory was later discarded in favor of a biochemical model.

Although Pavlov was a physiologist, he knew little of the operation of neurons. He explained his conditioned-response experiments in this way: the sound of the bell triggered electrical activity in the form of a wave in the brain. Because this wave reached the brain center controlling salivation just as this center began to operate at the sight of food, Pavlov reasoned that new electrical pathways would be established between the hearing center and the salivary center. Further ringing of the bell would then act to put the salivary control center into operation, even without the stimulus of food.

According to W. Grey Walter, who worked with Pavlov when the latter came to England, the Russian researcher showed no desire to look behind the scenes. "He was not in the least interested in the mechanism of cerebral events; they just happened, and it was the happening and its consequences that interested him, not how they happened."

Pavlov would have had much difficulty in trying to investigate the actual mechanism of the "electrical waves" he theorized. As yet little had been done in measuring the electrical activity of the brain, and it was not until 1909 that the noted physiologist Ramon y Cajal detected the presence of closed circuits of neurons in the brain. Soon a Canadian psychologist, D. O. Hebb, used Cajal's neuron loops to theorize an assembly of cortical neurons as the real engram.

A Network of Switches

Regardless of the memory theory he subscribes to, every scientist deals with the same components, switches, wires, and other parts. We have seen that there are in general three types of neurons, or nerve cells: the afferent, or sensory neurons; the efferent, or motor cells; and the internunciatory, or associative cells. Memory seems to rely on huge numbers—billions—of these associative cells. The neurons, then, seem to be the circuitry of the memory, collections of switches that can with much justification be compared to those in a computer, yet at the same time are assembled and arranged with incomprehensible cunning in the brain.

Communications theory is quite well developed, and experts in this field have devised efficient codes for carrying information.

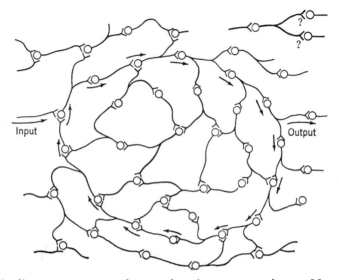

This diagram represents the reverberating memory theory. Memory trace is shown by arrows; however, explanation of why electrochemical impulses would follow this particular neuronal circuit is not clear.

Binary codes easily convey information through electronic computers, expressing it in ones and zeros that correspond to the two states of the multiplicity of switches in the machine. Because the neuron is an on-off switch, with important and awesome differences, a code similar to the binary code may be used in memory.

The memory of so basic an item of information as our name and phone number obviously requires dozens of digits or bits of information. A lifetime of memories adds up to how many bits? Ralph Gerard guesses a "frame" of experience at 1/10 second and a thousand bits of information per frame. Thus some 15 trillion bits would be perceived in a lifespan of seventy years. This is about fifteen hundred times the number of nerve cells in the brain. No one knows, of course, how many bits of information are stored in human memory; and experts have estimated anywhere from 1,500,000 bits to 12^{21} bits: 1,000,000,000,000,-000,000,000, or a billion trillion!

Fortunately the brain *is* equipped with billions of switches.

More fortunately for us—though not for the engineer trying to fathom the mystery of the human brain—many if not most of these billions of neurons are connected not just with two others, but with as many as tens of thousands of other neurons. If as few as one million neurons were interconnected with each other, there would be $10^{2,783,000}$ possible combinations, a number that probably exceeds all the coded memories of everybody.

The memory trace, the neural circuit or pathway, comprises a network of neurons. As a way of refreshing our memories at this point, we recall that neurons consist of a nucleus within a cell body that also comprises one or more dendrites and a single axon. The dendrites are the inputs to the neuron "switch." The axon is the output. Simply stated, a stimulus reaches the neuron through a dendrite. If this stimulus is sufficient to "fire" the

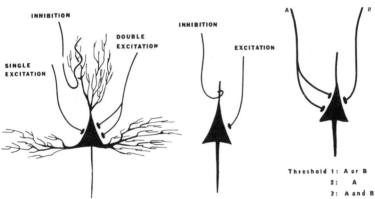

Diagrams of neuron stimulation, showing inhibitory and excitatory synapses. At right is logical analysis of neuron with varying thresholds of excitation.

neuron, an electrochemical occurrence takes place within the cell body. An action potential, or electrochemical wave, moves out along the axon and is in turn communicated to the dendrites of other neurons in the nerve network. There are several basic network configurations into which neurons are organized. Although axons do not branch, neurons do "arborize," or form tree-like configurations. Typical configurations are convergence, divergence or dispersion, delay lines, and feedback or amplifying circuits.

Synapses can be excitatory or inhibitory. According to Sir John Eccles, inhibitory phenomena are highly developed in the brain and play a major role in memory. He feels that "finely tuned responses" can be regarded as "the chiseling away of random and diffuse output into a more specific output." In other words, learning may be more a matter of curbing circuits than of creating them.

Concerning electrochemical transmission, McDougall noted:

> It is highly probable that the chief resistances to the passage of the current lie at the synapses, or junctions between neurons, and that the essential effect of the passage of the current is a diminution of these synaptic resistances.

Today's physiologists agree with McDougall's educated guess concerning the great importance of the synapse in the transmission of signals through neurons. Furthermore, scientists now believe that chemical synaptic transmission adds an amplifying mechanism, which may be a hundredfold, to the "switch." The chemical acetylcholine released at the synapses permits ionic permeability changes so that only 1 percent of the electrical charge normally necessary will complete a circuit.

A single neuron may have as many as ten thousand synapses. Most of these are dendritic "spines" and are excitatory in nature. "Body" synapses, involving the soma of the neuron, are inhibitory. There are not thought to be any synaptic connections between dendrites in the brain, although some have been found in the spinal cord of fish.

The nerve network theory can be compared to the electrical or electronic circuits in the computer. Memory, according to this concept, stems from fixed pathways established in certain parts of the brain. This idea appeals because of its simplicity and because it lends itself to the localization of memory. Certain parts of the brain store visual images; other parts hold the auditory, olfactory, tactile, and other memories. It is like the rigidly wired circuits of a home lighting system. If you push a certain switch, the associated light goes on or off. Dr. J. Z. Young of the Department of Anatomy at University College, London, proposes a similar circuitry in the memory of a living thing—the octopus. Chosen because its neurons are large and lend themselves to laboratory investigation, the octopus has been carefully studied with regard to its responses to various stimuli.

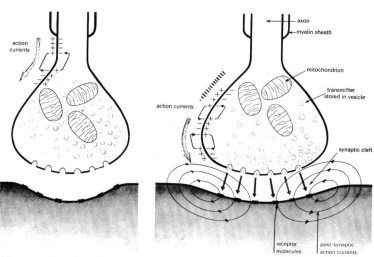

Message impulse is transmitted across the synaptic cleft, from one neuron to the next, by a process that draws on the electrochemical energy of the impulse, or action potential, to produce a transmitter substance that diffuses across the gap. Alternative theory of memory proposes structural and biochemical changes occurring within the synapse in response to incoming stimuli.

The octopus is trained to recognize certain shapes and to respond properly to them by, for example, such actions as attacking for food and retreating from pain. Dr. Young suggests that during the training period neural switches are set in the optic lobe of the creature's brain. The "food" symbol, recognized by the brain, triggers the attack switches; the "enemy" symbol triggers the retreat switches, and the motor nerves act accordingly.

This is admittedly a simple example of a memory trace, but the theory permits extension of this elementary switching to include the complexities inherent in remembering by heart all of a Shakespearean play, a long and complicated musical composition, or what we wore to our birthday party at age five.

It takes much faith to believe that detailed memories can be captured and retained in a network of neurons so small that we can't see them unless we use microscopes. Yet we take for granted a Rachmaninoff concerto reproduced flawlessly in stereophonic high fidelity and "memorized" in the squiggles and grooves of an LP record or on an eight-track Mylar tape. Nor do we give more than a passing thought to a color television show whose basic reality is nothing more than a modulated microwave frequency that we could not possibly see as it really is.

Dynamic Memory What we have described so far is a "static" memory trace. The pathway is there but not used until it is triggered by some initiating action on the part of the brain. Another school of thought held that the process must not be static but dynamic, that the memory persisted, ringing constantly in the mind. Forbes and Lorente de No introduced the idea of reverberatory activity and recurrent circuits in the 1920s, and Rashevsky, an American scientist, was a staunch proponent of the dynamic or "reverberating memory" theory. More recently, in 1960 Verzeano and Negishi, using groups of four microelectrodes, have ascertained the firing pattern of a small network of cells over a period of time. These patterns indicate recirculation of electrical activity through the network, although for only short durations.

Physiologists have known for a long time that electrochemical occurrences are involved in the functioning of the brain. Fritsch and Hitzig showed that an electrical impulse applied to the brain of a dead man caused movement in the body. More recently, it has been demonstrated that the application of an appropriate electrical pulse to various parts of the brain calls up memories of past events. The electric wave then is not merely incidental to some other controlling factor involved but is a major factor in memory. The incoming stimulus from a sensory nerve causes an electrochemical pulse or potential or wave to move along the axon of an associative cell. This pulse must

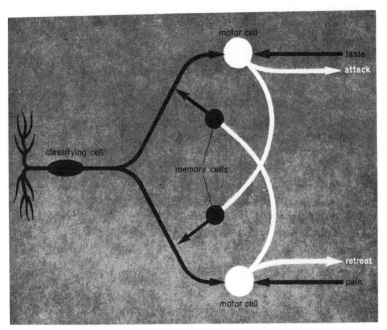

Components of a hypothetical single memory unit—a mnemon. The classifying cell records the occurrence of a special class of events. It has two possible outputs, which can produce two possible motor events, attack or retreat. The system is biased to one of these (in the octopus it would be attack). Following this action, signals indicating its results arrive and either reinforce what has been done or produce the opposite action. Collateral connections of these motor cells then activate special small cells, which produce inhibitory transmitter and close the unused pathway. These latter cells could be called memory cells.

branch to other neurons through their dendrites, and part of the dynamic theory is that a circulating or reverberating pulse is set up in a completed circuit. Such reverberating or "ringing" circuits are produced in electronic equipment. In fact, an early computer memory called a delay line was truly a reverberating circuit containing information that could be extracted as needed.

Sherrington, among others, saw the brain as an "enchanted loom" on which patterns played ceaselessly. Memory was a humming, dynamic process with millions of contemporaneous traces or circuits looping through myriad pathways of the brain, overlapping each other in many cases. However, the reverberating memory circuit was seriously challenged when researchers froze the brains of animals for months at temperatures cold

Weaving back and forth between two spherical mirrors, this laser beam travels nearly two miles. The beam forms an optical "delay line" on which information may be stored. In time, devices like this may store telephone numbers, billing information, or other data for telephone central offices.

enough to stop all organic motion and then demonstrated that, when the brains were thawed, the memory seemed to survive. At least the brain produced electroencephalograms almost identical to those produced prior to the freezing process.

A synthesis of the two opposing theories has evolved slowly. Perhaps, some say, there are two kinds of memory: a short-term memory that *is* effected by a reverberating circuit, and the more permanent long-term memory in which the pulses no longer circulate continuously but have established a pathway so that upon demand the proper circuit is again set in motion. An analogy would be a sudden flood that sent water coursing through new terrain seeking a channel for itself. Perhaps a second flood would carve slightly different channels, but eventually a definite route would be opened up so that villagers could avoid the river itself when it flooded. Here is the memory trace of the long-term variety.

Another analogy would be the negotiation of a maze in which each twist in the path had been marked, or perhaps roadblocks had been set up so that only the proper turns could be taken. The footprints of the people negotiating the maze might also gradually wear a trail in the ground. Regardless of the precise mechanism, the concept is the same. Frequent use of the same pathways and gates eventually sets them in the proper position so that when a course is to be run, the path is automatic.

Gerard suggests the mechanism of fixing a reverberating trace into a permanent one. At fifty reverberations per second, in half an hour a hundred thousand cycles of the trace will have been laid down. And anything that runs a course a hundred thousand times should leave quite a trail! He describes the fixing of a permanent memory trace this way:

> Early in any learning experience, as the organism's actions fail to solve the problem and eliminate the disturbing input, there is great central irradiation; muscle tension is increased, there is generalized contraction of irrelevant as well as of the desired muscles, autonomic discharges occur, tension and attention are intense, the "consciousness of necessity" is high, and many neurons in cortex and deep centers show electrical activity on mass or microelectrode recording. Later, when learned responses have been established,

general radiation disappears, muscles relax, there is little tension and maybe not even attention, habituation is evident from performance and experiences, and electric activity has disappeared from all neurons except those specifically involved in the response. With errors or other kinds of emergency situations, the electrical activity and other signs of irradiation promptly return. As an action is learned and certain paths through the nervous system become canalized, irradiation is eliminated.

In the octopus the removal of the *verticalis* complex of the brain has been found to prevent retention of memory on a long-term basis. Short-term memory in the octopus seems to be a function of the optic lobes. It is thought that the *verticalis* complex somehow presents visual memories again, from within, and thus brings about the permanent change needed for long-term memory.

Distributed Memory Hitzig, who pioneered research into the electrochemical activity of the brain, argued for "distributed" memory:

> I agree that the intelligence—better called the store of ideas—is to be sought in all parts of the cortex—better again to say all parts of the brain. . . .

Later researchers would add the dynamic concept and propose a memory theory totally opposed to the fixed memory trace. Propounded most forcefully by Karl Lashley, the dynamic concept, simply stated, is that memory persists not as a sequence or network of switches set in fixed positions like the runways and gates of a maze but as a continuously moving, overall pattern of activity that encompasses not merely localized areas of the brain but most of the brain. Indeed, some theorists extend the network of the brain pattern to include the motor nerves and perhaps even the muscles themselves. One hypothesis envisions memory so widely distributed that it is not the neurons themselves but the surrounding tissues that form the network.

Lashley cited the phenomenon of watching a moving object with the eyes fixed in one direction. For him this phenomenon ruled out the notion that certain neurons must handle certain jobs. Instead, Lashley theorized a *pattern* that may operate anywhere in the brain, in different places at different times. It is difficult to explain what controls the pattern; however, he argued not only for a distributed memory but for "equipotentiality" as well, because he felt that all neurons were equally fitted for any memory trace and were probably so used at different times—or even at the same time for totally different traces. Lashley suggested two possibilities for such memory circuits: "potential gradients" in cortical electrical fields and "resonance patterns" in neural loops.

Despite the difficulties attendant upon the distributed memory theory, it is thriving again today. Dr. E. C. Zeeman of Warwick University, who based his work on the concept that thought itself is a dynamic rather than a static process, suggested in 1966 that memory is an overall changing state of all the brain's neurons. His arguments relied on the mathematics of topology. And in 1967 Professor H. C. Longuet-Higgins of Edinburgh University's Department of Machine Intelligence suggested a "hologram" theory of dynamic memory.

A conventional hologram uses laser light to illuminate a special film and to produce an image. Many images may be superimposed on the same film and produced as desired by varying the laser light, although one frequency of light will show "ghosts" of all the other images in addition to the associated one. There are also holograms of sound, called holophones. Longuet-Higgins thinks brain cells might act in a way analogous to the visual images on the hologram film. In response to different signals from the brain, associative neurons in linked chains or nets provide certain responses, much like what are called networks of coupled resonators in electronic circuitry. Stimulating one such response might set off a learned chain of sequential responses; thus the same neurons could be involved in many different memory networks. A similar idea, calling for networks of neurons behaving as "loosely coupled oscillators," was advanced some years ago by J. W. S. Pringle.

Since such dynamic circuits could be quiescent until triggered by the proper signals, they may escape the seeming death blow that the brain-freezing experiments dealt earlier distributive theories.

Growing New Memories   The neuron is not a static entity but has a high rate of metabolism and may renew its protoplasmic content three times daily. Here is how Gerard describes the physical action of the neuron:

> A neuron, at least in tissue culture, is a restless entity. It shows the usual swellings and churnings of other cells and its processes thrust out and retract pseudopodial branches and terminations unceasingly.

One theory of memory states that neurons grow new synaptic connections under the influence of sensory stimulation. In fact, an extension of this theory explains why old people have trouble remembering new things—their neurons are already so loaded

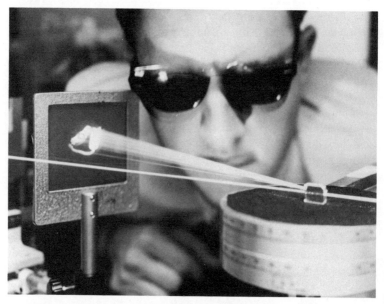

A scientist reconstructs a holographic image stored in a lithium niobate crystal. As many as a thousand different hologram images can be stored in a single crystal simply by rotating the crystal a fraction of a degree for each new hologram. The hologram memory theory is analogous to this optical device.

with dendritic "spines" that new growth cannot be accomplished. Electric shock treatment of those with mental problems is thought to destroy some of these spines and allow formation of newer, "healthier" connections. A companion theory says that forgetting is occasioned by the degeneration of nerve fibers. Unfortunately for the growth theory, however, more dendritic spines are observed on fetal or newborn neuronal material than on aging neurons.

Roger Sperry does not agree with the growth theory. He feels that because cells are differentiated chemically from the outset, the proper connections for "instinctive memory" are assured. Sperry says, "As far as I know, among all the synapses that have been observed in the history of neurology, not one of them has yet been demonstrated to have been implanted by learning."

No Final Answer   There have been, and continue to be, various memory theories describing memory as a fixed network or circuit of neurons (either static or dynamic), a pattern capable of existing in different parts of the brain, or both these mechanisms. Other theories advance ideas like the actual growth of new connections between neurons and explain that memory loss with age stems from degeneration of these connections. Despite many clever and plausible analogies with computers and other electronic circuitry, it is obvious that no scientist is satisfied with present nerve network theories of memory. The best minds among physiologists, psychologists, logicians, and physicists, to name a few, have arrived at no final answers in the search for memory. Memory is defined by a cynic as that which helps us worry. And much of the worry is over memory itself. Roger Sperry, one of those most knowledgeable in the field of memory, points up some of the problems:

> Not only is it quite possible that we may already have the answer to the memory trace, but, perhaps more important, we probably would not recognize the answer today if we did have it—even if it were served to us on a silver platter fully outlined, physiologically, and complete with a sheet of instructions for molecular analysis. The reason is that there are so many unknowns between neural engram at the one level and memory, as

we know it, at the behavioral level. The problem of the anatomy of memory right now is not so much to find the answer but to find the problem. To formulate the problem of the engram clearly, we have to work our way down to it. In a sense, we are looking for a secret code of an unknown code of subjective meaning and information, which in itself is pretty insubstantial stuff. We have our images, our memories, our impressions of last year's vacation and whatnot, or we see new movement skills or new responses, but those, of course, don't translate very easily into engrams.

Chapter Nine

COMPUTERS AND MEMORY

James R. Newman, in *The World of Mathematics,* says that the computer is less like a man than is an amoeba, but nevertheless it is more like a brain than any machine has ever been before. He goes on to say that the computer is close enough to a brain to make men shiver and then ask if one might gain knowledge of the structure of the brain by comparing restricted aspects of its input and output with the input and output of computers, whose structure is known.

It can be argued that the question-and-answer games with computers stem from tricks of programming and that machines that play chess or tic-tac-toe are likewise exhibiting trivial stunts that are no indication of true memory. However, the notion has intrigued not only those associated with computers but also the physiologists. As John Von Neumann put it:

> Natural organisms are, as a rule, much more complicated and subtle, and therefore much less well understood in detail, than are artificial automata. Nevertheless, some regularities which we observe in the organization of the former may be quite instructive in our thinking and planning of the latter; and conversely, a good deal of our experiences and difficulties with our artificial automata can be to some extent projected on our interpretations of natural organisms.

Some years ago the British mathematician A. M. Turing proposed a test of the computer's ability to think. Imagine a game in which the participants remain in separate rooms and converse by means of typewritten messages. Here are some sample questions and answers Turing gives:

Q. Please write me a sonnet on the subject of the Forth Bridge.
A. Count me out on this one. I never could write poetry.
Q. Add 34957 to 70764.
A. (Pause about 30 seconds and then give as answer 105721.)
Q. Do you play chess?
A. Yes.
Q. I have K at my K1, and no other pieces. You have only K at K6 and R at R1. It is your move. What do you play?
A. (After a pause of 15 seconds) R-R8 mate.

Is the respondent a human being or a computer? Since Turing proposed this "imitation game," as he called it, the computer has demonstrated not only that it can do arithmetic and play chess, as Turing suggested, but that it can compose poetry as well. Two decades after Turing described his imitation game, it was played at M. I. T. between a young lady and an IBM computer. In the following excerpt, her conversation is in lower case letters, and the computer's responses are in capitals:

Dr. Arthur L. Samuel of IBM has played chess with a computer. As yet, the machine plays an indifferent game of chess but can beat master checkers players.

men are all alike
IN WHAT WAY
they're always bugging us about something or other
CAN YOU THINK OF A SPECIFIC EXAMPLE
well, my boy friend made me come here
he noticed that i'm depressed much of the time
I AM SORRY TO HEAR YOU ARE DEPRESSED
he's right. i am unhappy
DO YOU THINK COMING HERE WILL HELP YOU NOT
   TO BE UNHAPPY
i need some help, that much is clear
WHAT WOULD IT MEAN TO YOU IF YOU GOT SOME
   HELP
perhaps i could learn to get along with my mother
TELL ME MORE ABOUT YOUR FAMILY
my mother takes care of me
WHO ELSE IN YOUR FAMILY TAKES CARE OF YOU
my father
YOUR FATHER
you are like my father in some ways
WHAT RESEMBLANCE DO YOU SEE
you are not very aggressive but i don't think you want me to
   notice that
WHAT MAKES YOU THINK I AM NOT VERY AGGRESSIVE
you don't argue with me
WHY DO YOU THINK I DON'T ARGUE WITH YOU
you are afraid of me
DOES IT PLEASE YOU TO BELIEVE I AM AFRAID OF YOU
it pleases my father to think i am afraid of him
WHAT ELSE COMES TO MIND WHEN YOU THINK OF
   YOUR FATHER
bullies

Is the "doctor" a psychiatrist or a computer?

Digital Cousins   Man's heart is a pump, his kidneys
are filters, and his lungs are gas-exchange systems. As Descartes
pointed out, man is a machine, with levers, plumbing, and
chemical works throughout his body. It is hardly surprising that
attempts are made to equate the brain with some artificial
device, that man would try to explain the workings of his

memory by means of a calculator or computer. It is not an easy task, that of creating a brain model.

Von Neumann suggested that perhaps the only model of the brain is the brain itself, that its structure and operation are so complex that man can never construct an adequate model. Others go even further and state categorically that the human brain is so complicated that man can never hope to understand it. All these statements, of course, have not stopped other men from indulging their curiosity by probing deeply to learn the workings of memory.

There is a science called "bionics," a marriage of engineering and biology that works in both directions. By studying living mechanisms and the solutions of nature to many problems, engineers supposedly can construct better machines. Lighter structures, more efficient pumps, and more powerful thrust-producers are examples. On the other hand, by studying mechanical and other artificial devices, biologists can learn things about living systems. Bionics meets a worthy challenge in the brain.

The search for memory can go only so far in the living brain. In putting a finger on it, some have said, the thing itself is destroyed. Even the simplest living nervous systems are so complex that man can only infer how they operate. It is one thing to suspect that short-term memory stems from some sort of reverberating circuit in a network of neurons; proving this theory by mapping the network itself is as yet impossible. Even the most sophisticated electrical measurements and surgical work yield no working knowledge of the miracle of memory in the living brain. The design of better electronic or other computers from studies of the brain must rely on psychological inference or on the black-box approach rather than on physiological dissection and neuron circuit tracing. The remaining method is to reverse the picture and to attempt to map out the operation of human memory by constructing simple mechanical, electrical, or electronic models and by seeing whether they can perform functions the brain seems to perform.

There are two basic types of computer: analog and digital. The analog is a measuring device; a physical scale in the computer stands for the amount or quantity to be measured. A slide rule is an analog device—a length marked out on a flat surface represents a quantity. The gasoline gauge in your car is an analog device. Analog computers represent quantities with varying amounts of electrical voltage or with distances on a scale.

The digital computer is a counting device. Man's fingers gave the machine its name—fingers are digits, and toes may be added for more complex problems. Most high-speed electronic computers are digital devices because this system lends itself well to working mathematical and logical problems rapidly.

An Air Force engineer studies a complex biological problem on LANNET (Large Artificial Nerve NETwork). Problems include maze learning, the Pavlov conditioned response, perception, and response. This artificial brain contains 1,024 switches or "artificial neurons."

How about human memory—is it analog or digital? Perhaps surprisingly, the scientific concept of the brain is that of a digital computer. Although some see it as an analog apparatus, it is basically digital with some analog overtones or undertones involved in its circuitry.

In 1938 a young student at M. I. T. named Claude Shannon published a paper entitled "A Symbolic Analysis of Relay and Switching Circuits," which was destined to affect the design of electronic computers that were at that time only gleams in designers' eyes. The gist of Shannon's insight was that electrical and electronic circuitry, utilizing on-off switches, could best be described by Boolean, or two-valued logic. The computer to come would use Boolean logic; it would be a binary device using only two numbers in its arithmetic system: 1 and 0.

Dr. Claude E. Shannon conceived this electrical "mechanical mouse" with its man-made supermemory. Experiments with the mouse proved that a machine can, through a rote search pattern, establish a route through a maze by using the trial-and-error concept and that once established, the machine will travel the same route again without error. In a limited sense, this experiment proved that a machine has a "memory."

In 1943 a step forward in the study of neural mechanisms was made with the publishing of a paper by McCulloch and Pitts, "A Logical Calculus of the Ideas Immanent in Nervous Activity." The basis for this paper was the idea that *all* psychological phenomena, including memory, can be understood through the concept of two-valued logic. An on-off electrical switch is a two-valued logical device. With enough of these switches, even the most complex phenomena can be defined logically in a sort of "twenty questions" procedure. Anything that can be defined logically in words can also be defined by a neural network.

This logical approach to neuron function became known as the "McCulloch-Pitts neuron." The basic assumptions were as follows:

> The activity of the neuron is an all-or-none process. A certain fixed number of synapses must be excited within the period of latent addition in order to excite a neuron at any time, and this number is independent of previous activity and position on the neuron.
>
> The only significant delay within the nervous system is synaptic delay. The activity of any inhibitory synapse absolutely prevents excitation of the neuron at that time.
>
> The structure of the net does not change with time.

These two papers pointed out the compatibility of minds and machines and set the stage for the many investigations using computers to study memory, and vice versa, that followed.

The Computer's Memory

The notion of machines that can think dates back to the golems of the Old Testament, and the mechanist philosophers have long treated the body as a machine. Endowment of the computer with as human-sounding a capability as memory is more than anthropomorphism or pathetic fallacy. For the machine duplicates, at least crudely, some of the basic phenomena involved in man's reasoning processes. For example, the major parts of a computer are input, storage, arithmetic or logic, control, and output, components that are roughly comparable to man's perception, memory, decision-making, and motor responses.

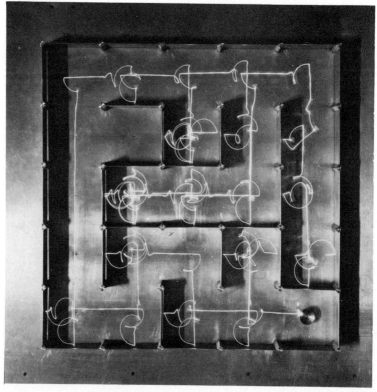

Time exposures show the path taken by Shannon's electrical mouse as it winds its way through the maze. The pattern on the left, made by attaching a small light to the mouse, shows the mouse's explorations on

A computer's input can use a variety of sense modes. Men have read by the Braille system for more than a century; Babbage's computer used a similar system, "feeling" messages in punched cards. Today there are more sophisticated machines that read electrically, magnetically, and even optically. Others can be operated by sounds and in some instances by human commands or questions. And there are computers whose input consists of smells that they compare, for recognition purposes, against a stored library of smells.

The concept of "thinking machines" causes many people to

its two-minute trip to the goal at the lower right. The pattern on the right shows what the mouse can do once it has made this exploration. Without a single false move, it goes directly to the goal in twelve to fifteen seconds.

react as they would to a bogeyman; some flatly deny such a possibility. However, certain computers seem to do what can be classed as thinking. The human brain evolved as a problem-solving organ; the computer was designed as a problem-solving machine. Computers do arithmetic and logic problems, sorting and filing, translating, information retrieval, process monitoring and control, and other things human beings once considered above the ability of machines.

About a century ago Babbage built two general classes of

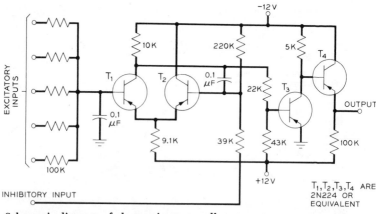

Schematic diagram of electronic nerve cell.

computers that were the forerunners of today's machines. These two classes contain parallels to living nervous systems. His first machine was called a "difference engine" because it solved problems by operating on fixed differences to set up tables desired by the operator. Setting the gears of the difference engine resulted in a mechanical, precise set of numbers to a prearranged series, a sort of reflex action. The response of the engine was built in and could not vary, just as the reflex action of a dog, a chicken, or a man does not vary. Tap yourself on the kneecap and your leg jerks in a well-known reflex action over which your conscious brain has no control, short of tying the leg down. Even then the muscles will strain obediently in trying to obey the reflex arc message.

Later Babbage envisioned what he called a "calculating engine" that would make the difference engine seem as primitive as single-celled creatures do compared with man. The calculating engine had a memory, the power of choice, and the ability to seek out answers to practically any problem.

Given a task, the engine could pick and choose among its memory, or store, for answers. If it did not find the information it needed, the engine would ring a bell to ask for additional data. Having worked out answers, it could store the parts of the problems, as "subroutines," that would be useful in solving other tasks, much as a pianist learns chords and runs or as a youngster memorizes his mathemetical tables and formulae.

Babbage was a century ahead of the technology needed to make his dream machines come true, and only in the middle 1940s did the electronic computer finally make its appearance. When it did come, however, its designers were amazed to find that Babbage had correctly predicted most of what they did. Today's computers are a synthesis of the two types devised by Babbage. There are two kinds of memory in computers, wired-in or instinctive memory and something that is more flexible and that may qualify, depending on one's definition, as learning. Although the other portions of the computer—the input and output, the mill or arithmetic-logic unit, and the control—are all fascinating subjects for further study, we will restrict ourselves here to computer memory systems, of which there are many.

The ubiquitous IBM card is recognized by nearly everyone now. At Christmas it appears as a festive card punched to spell season's greetings or curled into artistic shapes and sprayed bright colors to make a Yuletide decoration. Herman Hollerith first put the card to practical use doing arithmetic on the U.S. census in 1890. Prior to that, however, Babbage had used punched cards, and he in turn borrowed the idea from Jacquard and others who used them to "program" weaving looms once set up by painstaking hand operations.

Deceptively simple-looking, a computer card can nevertheless store a wealth of information. A single one can physically describe a person and catalog his social, financial, and educational status—at least when run through a compatible computer. But then a human engram, whatever it may be, is of little value until it too is played back through a sophisticated readout on call from a central control portion of the brain.

A stack of computer cards six inches high stores data on hundreds of people and is ready on short notice to give out that data. Memory is incorporated into the computer card by the simple process of punching holes at coded locations. A hole ten spaces from the left and five from the top represents a bit of information—brown hair or financial solvency or ability to teach second-year Spanish at the college level. Here is memory, stored in a thin sheet of cardboard a few inches long that looks nothing like the data it represents. To store on punched cards all the facts we have in our heads would result in a stack that would fill any warehouse and that would require many years for readout. When large amounts of information must be stored as computer memory, a newer and more sophisticated method is used. One method is magnetic tape.

These racks of tape reels form part of the memory of a large computer information-processing system.

We are familiar with sound stored on tape; a few feet of plastic film with a metallic coating so fine that we can't see it with the naked eye have committed to memory a fantastic number of notes, all of which can be recalled by passing the tape through a sensing head that converts the magnetic charges into electrical impulses of the proper magnitude and frequency to re-create faithfully what was recorded some time in the past. Computer tape is a higher density storage medium than punched cards, but to pack into tape reels the knowledge of even an average human being would still require a sizable storehouse.

Computer memories are also stored on magnetic discs, a system somewhat like phonograph records but similar to tape storage except for the physical shape of the storage medium. Discs have the advantage of being easier to search through for a particular bit of material. Although a tape must be run serially through the "read head" until the desired information is reached, the head may be quickly moved to reach a desired disc location, much as we manually position the needle of a phonograph over the desired grooves.

One very sophisticated computer memory used presently is the magnetic core. Tiny doughnuts of ferrite, a material capable of being instantly magnetized or demagnetized, are strung on wires carrying electrical current. When a ferrite core is electrically magnetized by a current in the wire, the core keeps this magnetism indefinitely because of its high retentivity, a property of ferrite.

Magnetic core "memory unit" of IBM 704.

The ferrite core is useful as a computer memory element because it is like a two-position switch. It is magnetized in one direction or the other, and this polarity can be detected by "sense wires." Thousands of cores are strung together in memory plane matrices, each core with a particular location or "address." Each location can be magnetized to be a binary 1 or 0, yes or no, on or off. This two-valve code is the basis of binary computer operation.

In a way analogous to a human being's memorizing of data, a magnetic core plane can be filled with information in the form of ones and zeros. When this information is desired, it can be requested and read out. In some cases this readout destroys the memory, but it is possible to make the stored information permanent in the cores. Here is a completely different kind of memory from the delay line or the magnetic tape. The delay line is dynamic or circulating and thus not practical to store forever. The magnetic tape is not fleeting; it goes to the other extreme and cannot easily be changed. True, it can be erased and retaught, but this is a crude process. The core memory, on the other hand, can easily be changed and is thus a very flexible storage system for information. The core memory is an electromagnetic system, in comparison with the electrochemical memory of the brain.

Dynamic Memory One early type of computer memory was the acoustic "delay line." In this system a sound wave was produced by a transducer in mercury or some other sound-conducting medium. At the far end of the delay line, the sound wave was picked up, converted to an electrical impulse, and fed back to where it started. Although this early memory is of only historic interest in the computer field, its similarity to the theory of the reverberating circuit in the brain is intriguing.

As long as power was supplied to the acoustic memory system, the stored information was available for recall on a cyclic schedule. Failure of power resulted in complete loss of memory, a condition that sometimes occurs in the living brain. The value of the delay line was as a short-term memory for small amounts of information, an interesting parallel to the concept of short-term memories in the brain. Another kind of continuously circulating current, or reverberating circuit, is that established in the "cryogenic" circuit. At very low temperatures electrical resistance fades away to almost nothing, and a current once set up continues to "ring" or persist.

Sixteen memory core planes provide computer with 4,096-word memory, and each word has a particular "address" or physical location.

Today the computer's memory is closely analogous to the static neural network theory proposed long ago by Hebb and others. Practical "dynamic" or "distributed" computer memories may be in the offing but they are not yet here.

Perceptrons   Computers are generally built not as brain models but to perform a particular task as artificial brains. There are, however, machines assembled specifically as models of the living brain. The term "brain model" has been defined as any theoretical system that attempts to explain the psychological functioning of a brain in terms of the known laws of physics and mathematics and the known facts of neuroanatomy and physiology. These models can be hypothetical or actual physical models constructed of mechanical and/or electrical and electronic components. The conventional digital computer is thought by some to be a brain model, but there are more sophisticated machines in this field. One of these is the "perceptron."

The black-box approach to comprehending the workings of the brain has been mentioned. In 1950 psychologist J. T. Culbertson formally spelled out this approach:

> Neuroanatomy and neurophysiology have not yet developed far enough to tell us the detailed interconnections holding within human or animal nets. . . . Consequently . . . we cannot start with specified nerve nets and then in a straightforward way determine their properties. Instead, it is the reverse problem which always occurs in dealing with organic behavior. We are given at best the vaguely defined properties of an unknown net and from these must determine what the structure of that net might possibly be. In other words we know, at least in a rough way, what the net does (as this appears in the behavior of the animal or man) and from this information we have to figure out what structure the net must have. . . . Our investigation passes through two stages. In the first stage—the behavioristic inquiry—we ignore the inner constituents, i.e., the nervous system and its activity, and concentrate our attention instead on the observable relations between the stimuli affecting the organism and the responses to which these stimuli give rise. . . . This makes the second stage, the functional inquiry—possible. Here, as Northrop says, we concentrate our attention on the inner (throughput) constituents of the system and point out the way in which the receptor cells, the central cells, and effector cells *could* be interconnected so that the input and output relations . . . would be discovered in stage 1.

Frank Rosenblatt, inventor of the "perceptron" form of brain model, finds fault, on a number of grounds, with this approach. One criticism is that it is impossible to have full knowledge of input and output relations for the behavior of an organism. Further, he feels that the inferred model would require impossible precision in hooking up its circuitry. The human brain, he points out, does not seem to be precisely "wired" and is able to function near perfection even though many of its parts are

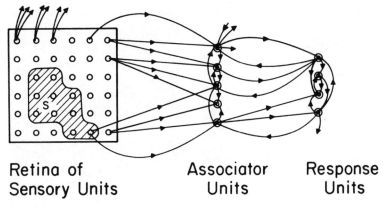

Retina of Sensory Units **Associator Units** **Response Units**

Simplified diagram of perceptron. Associator units compare with memory neurons.

imperfect. A similar failure rate in an electronic computer would cause breakdown almost immediately. Rosenblatt feels that, in order to come close to the performance of the living brain, a model with much more redundancy is needed. He is looking for new theories, new methods of operation rather than the simple on-off approach.

In 1957 Rosenblatt, at Cornell University, introduced the term and the concept of the perceptron. In Rosenblatt's words:

> Perceptrons are of interest because their study appears to throw light upon the biophysics of cognitive systems: they illustrate, in rudimentary form, some of the processes by which organisms, or other suitably organized entities, may come to possess "knowledge" of the physical world in which they exist, and by which the knowledge that they possess can be represented or reported when occasion demands.

Rosenblatt was primarily concerned with the problem of memory storage in the brain and in particular with the mechanism of "distributed memory," the equipotentiality phenomena reported by Dr. Karl Lashley and other specialists in the field of brain research. For a machine to remember it must first perceive something to be remembered, and Rosenblatt's model became known as a perceptron. A perceptron consists of sensory elements, asso-

University of Illinois "Numa rete" counts irregular-shaped objects and shows answers. There are four hundred photocells or sensory units.

ciative elements, and output units, components that compare roughly with the receptors, internuncial cells, and motor units in living brain systems.

An important difference between the perceptron and other brain models is the great freedom the machine is allowed in establishing connections between and among its "neurons" or basic elements. In other words, there is no built-in rule or "algorithm" in the perceptron. The perceptron receives stimuli from its environment and makes responses based on those stimuli. Its environment includes visual signals, or other sensory signals, plus the actions of a human experimenter who "teaches" the machine by reinforcement. The first perceptron to be built was Mark I.

Mark I consisted of a "retina" of four hundred photocells arranged in a grid of twenty cells on a side. Wires from the photocells were connected to 512 association units in random fashion instead of in a pattern that would guarantee a certain response. Finally, connections were made, again on a random basis, between association units and response units, with up to forty connections between each response unit and the associator units.

The Mark I perceptron was "taught" the alphabet by placing

large block letters before its retina of photocells and monitoring its reaction. Because of the electrical circuits that were actuated by the photocells, a response was given by the motor units. If this response was right, no correction was applied by the teacher. If it was in error, the teacher applied a correction to the motor-driven potentiometers that connected the association units to the response units and in effect weakened the connection for incorrect responses and strengthened it for correct responses.

Two classical kinds of training are given to perceptrons. The first, error-correction training, applies a correction only to wrong responses. The second, forced learning, gives a correction after each trial regardless of the perceptron's response. Interestingly, it was found that error-correction, analogous to punishment for failure, produced a faster rate of learning. The rod seemed to work as well with the perceptron as with the child, a psychological result Rosenblatt was pleased to find in his machine. Training was also given in which the *teacher* made some errors. Surprisingly, the perceptron did as well as when the trainer taught perfectly. Training was also given in situations where the environmental background was noisy, that is, in which interference was present.

In a computer with wired-in learning, removal of one or a few components results in destruction or degradation of the machine's memory. However, when Rosenblatt performed, by disconnecting large segments of association units, the equivalent of surgical removal of portions of a living brain, his perceptron still functioned fairly well. With half its association cells removed, it still retained about 95 percent of its original memory. Removal of three-fourths of the association units left the perceptron with about 90 percent of its memory, and with all but one-eighth of its "brain" excised it could still recognize more than 75 percent of the characters presented to it! This performance resembles that of living brains from which parts are surgically removed. Perceptron engineers feel that this experiment indicates that the random wiring of the perceptron is similar to the neuron networks in biological systems.

The perceptron performed the function Rosenblatt wished in that it proved itself a "general pattern-recognition device." Although a far simpler machine could be constructed to recognize specific objects, a perceptron has the ability to discriminate over a broader area. For instance, it can recognize letters in different locations, in positions other than erect ones, and in various nonstandard type faces. In addition, it can operate even with most of its connections broken. Here is a machine with something of the general abilities of living systems. Although conventional electronic computer operation depends on the absolute reliability of components and has led to fantastic demands for quality control, the human brain seems able to do an excellent job even with many unreliable components. Redundancy, the use of many more components than normally needed, seems to aid in this reliability.

This redundancy also makes possible "parallel operation," rather than series or sequential circuits. Most electronic computers are serial in nature, meaning that all calculations must run through the same circuits, one after the other. Some newer machines have parallel operation to the extent that a few tasks are being performed simultaneously, but in the living brain there is a multiplicity of parallel operations because of the great number of components. An analogy is having a hundred mathematicians working on a problem, each concentrating on a single aspect. If each is in an isolated room and is given the problem only when the man before him has completed his task, the problem will obviously take longer to solve than if all the men are in the same room and are given the problem at the same time. Each can begin working on his portion at once and therefore cut the time required for solution.

In addition to the perceptron, Rosenblatt and his colleagues at Cornell built "Tobermory," a perceptron designed to accept not visual images but auditory signals. Speech recognition is a more complex task than learning the letters of the alphabet. Tobermory consisted of sixteen hundred sensory units, a thousand association units, and twelve response units. Furthermore, because entire word recognition was needed in addition to recognition of basic sounds or "phonemes," additional detectors, response comparators, and integration switches were required.

Raytheon Company engineers have also built an auditory perceptron, named "Cybertron." It was taught to recognize words and also sonar sounds for possible use in underwater detection work. Profiting by the experience of the Mark I, Cybertron was taught by a "goof button" that the teacher pushed each time the machine erred.

In Rosenblatt's view, then, the brain and its component memory will turn out to be not a simple, wired-in learning computer with rigorously fixed connections but a much more subtle, sophisticated, and complex biological computer. Rosenblatt had this to say about the purpose of his perceptrons:

> Perceptrons are not intended to serve as detailed copies of any actual nervous systems. They are simplified networks, designed to permit the study of lawful relationships between the organization of a nerve net, the organization of its environment, and the "psychological" performance of which the network is capable. Perceptrons might actually correspond to parts of more extended networks in biological systems; in this case, the results obtained will be directly applicable. More likely, they represent extreme simplification of the central nervous system, in which some properties are exaggerated, others suppressed. In this case, successive perturbations and refinements of the system may yield a closer approximation.

In 1963 Rosenblatt proposed an advanced model for long-term sequential memory in the brain. This paper was delivered at the Computer and Information Sciences Symposium and gave an idea of the ambitiousness of Rosenblatt's design. The following are the "primary phenomena" that he felt should be explained by a satisfactory model:

1. Ability to recapitulate past experience in proper temporal order.
2. Selective recall, effects of "cognitive set," attention, and suggestion.

3. "Free association" (dreams, transitions and jumps between remembered events).
4. Retention and subsequent recall of originally "unnoticed" events.
5. Poor memory for sequences with low diversity (e.g., strings of digits), in contrast to sequences of nonrepetitive words.
6. Modification of stored information.
7. Effect of practice on accuracy of sequential recall.
8. Effects of "reinforcement" (pleasure, pain, reward, punishment) on memory.
9. Forgetting (transient and permanent).
10. "Repression," psychogenic amnesia, and subsequent recovery of memory.
11. Heightened accessibility of memory under hypnosis.
12. Posthypnotic suggestion.
13. Extra-high stability of early memory.
14. Low stability of recent memory in senility.
15. Lapse of memory during sleep or unconsciousness.
16. Retrograde amnesia (due to shock, cold, concussion, epileptic convulsion).
17. Recovery from retrograde amnesia in original temporal order.
18. Consolidation time (brief period following an event during which shock or trauma leads to irrevocable loss of memory).
19. Hallucinatory recall of sequences under temporal lobe stimulation.
20. Effects of localized lesions and electrical stimulation in aphasia, agnosia, and related disorders.
21. Distributed memory and functional equivalence of cortical regions.
22. Incapacity for retention of new experiences, without interference with recall of old experience, temporary memory, and motor learning, following hippocampal lesions.

Perhaps the only model that will meet these stringent criteria is, as John Von Neumann said, the brain itself!

Rosenblatt has continued his work on models of the brain, turning his attention to biochemical rather than electrical or electronic analogs. In 1967 he proposed a biochemical model, and his ideas were based on the recent promising work on memory transfer in animals. These ideas will be discussed in a later chapter.

Memory As More Than "Playback"   It is probable that the memory learns shortcut methods for storing information and for solving problems using that information. For example, memorizing a rule for multiplication is more efficient than memorizing all the possible arithmetical products. These shortcut methods lead us into what is called insight and concept, the most permanent kinds of memory. Here we see the appeal of the distributed memory theory of Lashley. Many of our complex memories are built up of "standard" subroutines or "loops" analogous to a computer program. A number of such loops may be involved, and some may be used more than once in a complete memory. One memory trace may be for dwellings and may contain a rough outline or configuration of what a house is. Colors might be in another trace or series of traces; textures and materials likewise may constitute still another category. In remembering a particular cabin in the mountains, for example, we may call on a number of widely differing memory categories: size, color, texture, smell, material. Also, in what sort of background is it? Given a thousand such building blocks, the brain could assemble countless thousands of completed images.

Complicating the problem is the fact that a variety of senses may be involved in a single memory. It may be necessary to recall how a person looks, sounds, smells, and feels. Food may involve looks, taste, smell, and touch, and in case of some cereals, even sound. These and other considerations prompted Rosenblatt to seek answers in his perceptron model rather than in a more conventional computer.

Physicist Heinz von Foerster of the University of Illinois challenges the idea of the memory as a table of stored bits of information. For analogy he uses the idea of printing multiplication tables on sheets of notebook paper. For multiplying up to 100×100 only a single sheet of paper is needed. But for ten-digit numbers he shows that a book 10^{15} centimeters thick will be required—a calculation that works out to something like a hundred times the distance from the earth to the sun. A librarian moving at the speed of light, says von Foerster, would require an average of half a day to look up a single answer in this mathematical memory. Obviously a simpler mechanism is needed, he says, and he suggests that the brain is not a "storehouse for a giant table" but a calculator or computer that works out solutions from a minimum of stored data.

For von Foerster the memory is a computer that must learn by experience the operations required of it:

> In looking for mechanisms that can be made responsible for the property of memory, I strongly suggest that we not look upon this system as if it were a recording device. Instead, I have proposed looking at this system as if it were a computer whose internal organization changes as a result of its interaction with an environment that possesses some order. The changes of the internal organization of this computer take place in such a way that some constraints in the environment which are responsible for its orderliness are mapped into the computer's structure. This system reveals itself as memory and permits the system to function as an inductive reference computer.

Von Foerster points out that because some 10^{20} bits of information are necessary to specify the connection of the ten billion neurons, and only half that number of bits are in a single egg cell, the network of the brain cannot be completely spelled out genetically.

Model for a Brain   The computer-memory analogy is perhaps not so farfetched as the timid would prefer to believe. Computers make use of the various circuitry, interconnections, delay lines or dynamic circuits, and digital-logic techniques discussed in connection with possible human memory mechanisms. The perceptron seems an especially attractive analog to the brain. Surely a cross-fertilization of ideas will bring benefits to both disciplines, electronic and biological. Just as surely, however, no computer scheme—from the early approaches of McCulloch and Pitts and Shannon to the recent and sophisticated self-adapting systems—offers anything approaching a real answer to the functioning of the brain and memory. For the brain is not just electrical, electronic, or electromechanical. Much of its operation is chemical in nature and so subtle and wonderful that no logic diagram, network of semiconductors, or computer program can hope to describe it. In the next chapter we will begin to consider these chemical aspects.

Chapter Ten

THE MOLECULAR THEORY OF MEMORY

An early text on biology describes the "memory" of linseed oil, which turns gummy when exposed to light. On the first brief exposure the change may be so slight as to be unobservable. However, subsequent exposures cause the oil to change more rapidly than if it had not been exposed previously. Thus the oil is said to have "remembered" its past experience and to behave differently because of it. Trivial as this tribute to oil may sound, the chemistry underlying it is the basis for many of the newer biochemistry texts treating the molecular theory of memory.

When the French physiologist Richard Semon in 1904 advanced his theory of the memory "engram," he suggested that it was chemical. For most of the intervening time the engram has generally been considered an electrical pathway rather than a chemical state. However, in recent years there have been increasing reminders that the brain is not an electrical or electronic computer but a chemical computer. The molecular biochemical theory of memory is part of this new approach, although the approach is not really new at all, of course.

We have seen that dynamic theories of memory are not well substantiated and that recent experiments seem to discredit such concepts as the "reverberating circuit," whereby an electric charge whirs through a network of neurons much as some early computer memories stored information as an echo or vibration in a cylinder of mercury or by some other circulatory method.

In 1950 psychologist Ward Halstead at the University of Chicago suggested that the memory trace might be a molecular change in the nucleic acids within a single neuron. The bio-chemical theory of memory is at the same time a molecular theory, because the discovery of DNA and RNA as molecular genetic blueprints converted biochemistry to a molecular pursuit.

About the same time Ralph W. Gerard of the University of Michigan reported that chilling hamsters to 40 degrees Fahrenheit stopped the electrical pulses from their brains. But when the hamsters were warmed, he found that they had not forgotten any of the things they had learned prior to the temperature drop. More recently, Japanese scientists froze a cat brain for six months and then established the fact that, when warmed, it produced electrical pulses similar to those produced before it was frozen. Brain activity also survives a variety of other attacks, such as shock, electroconvulsive therapy, glucose starvation, drugs, and so on. Purely dynamic explanations of memory have therefore been suspect in recent years. The mechanism seems to hinge on something more stable. Gerard wrote:

> Another mechanism enjoying some current popularity is chemical. Since every type of cell of every individual of every species has its own chemical personality, and since this differentiation of cell depends on proteins, the specificity of memory might be due to changes in nerve proteins. Each trace could be limited to one or a few molecules in an end-bulb of a neuron. The body cells that manufacture and release antibodies against invading organisms "learn," as we know, from experience. When typhoid proteins, for instance, enter the body the first time, antibodies are produced slowly in small amounts. But years later, when almost no antibody remains in the blood, a new invasion by this specific protein is met by a prompt and vigorous release of antibody that nips the disease before it gets started.

> It is far from explained just how the passage of nerve impulses would alter protein molecules at a synapse, or how, in turn, an altered protein composition would aid or hinder the passage of a nerve impulse. Yet some such chemical mechanism cannot be discarded, for nerves and synapses can be highly specific and change their specificity. . . .

Pioneers like Ramon y Cajal had necessarily treated memory at the cell level, and for some memory researchers the advent of

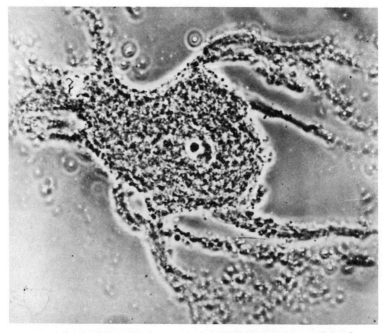

A neuron from the vestibular nucleus in the brain stem, enlarged two thousand diameters. Black dots are synaptic knobs.

molecular theory, DNA, RNA, etc., made no basic change in the neuronal network idea but simply added a further complexity. The nerve net was affected to some extent by molecular bio-chemistry, but it would be too "reductionistic" to seek memory below the cell level. Surely memory could not reside in mere components of a cell—in the "molecules of memory" as they popularly came to be called. However, others proclaimed that the memory molecule was not reductionist at all but was the true site, as Semon had proposed so long ago, of the trace or engram. Gerard made an interesting analogy:

> Partial engrams—of percepts, images and acts—are built onto larger ones—concepts, imaginings and skills—much as a small assortment of amino-acids is used to build a limitless variety of proteins. In the same way, learning goes from letters to words to

sentences, with plateaus of achievement at each larger unit; and bits of information become aggregated into larger "chunks" so that a greater quantity can be handled in a given time.

Since RNA is known to be part of genetic coding, a kind of blueprint of inheritance and a building guide for cells, the idea that it might also be involved in memory was natural. The genetic code is a memory of a sort, a built-in memory that controls the growth of cells. One researcher, Dr. D. Ewen Cameron at McGill University gave elderly human patients doses of yeast RNA and claimed that their memories improved. Cameron noted that many of his patients who suffered from poor memory had higher-than-average amounts of RNase in their blood. Suspecting that the RNase was adversely affecting their brain RNA, Cameron fed the patients large amounts of yeast RNA. RNase levels were lowered, and in patients who were not seriously regressed when treatment began, Cameron reported significant improvement in memory.

DNA and RNA   Among those who were intrigued by the possibility of a molecular base for memory was the eminent Swedish biologist Holger Hydén at the University of Sweden in Goteburg. As it was established that DNA in an egg cell encoded or "remembered" the physical characteristics of its ancestors and directed the assembling of a like being, Hydén and his colleagues wondered whether current memories might not be stored in a similar fashion. The genetic code of DNA stored structural memories, instincts, reflexes. Why not a similar mechanism for experiential memories? Hydén looked to RNA for the storehouse, rather than to DNA. His theory was as simple as it was bold: An incoming sensory stimulus synthesized a specific "macromolecule" or giant molecule in the appropriate area of memory.

Here is how Hydén phrased his question:

The neurons and glia contain a considerable amount of RNA, and it seemed reasonable to ask if a change by use in the nervous system could consist of lasting chemical changes, and if memory resides in the spatial arrangements of the molecules of the brain, and if RNA and proteins and the rate of production, perhaps, could be the substrate for learning.

Hydén went to work in his laboratories to test his idea.

It was known that stimulation of neurons artificially could result in the production of an increase in RNA in the nerve cell. This stimulation could be in the form of either electrical or chemical stimulation. For example, Hydén and a colleague demonstrated in 1947 that a substance later identified as 1, 3, 3, tricyano, 2-amino propene (TRIAP) produced a remarkable increase of RNA and protein in the Deiter's cells of rabbits. Interestingly, this compound was later found to stimulate regeneration of legs on newts and to speed the recovery of animals with crushed legs.

In later experiments G. P. Talwar in Delhi showed that exposure to light of an animal reared in darkness resulted in an

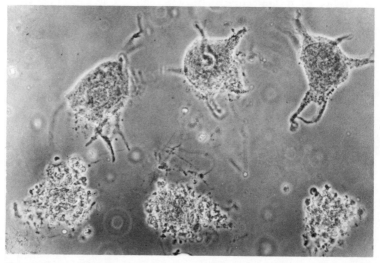

Fresh nerve cells plus the neuroglial cells that originally surrounded each cell.

increase in protein synthesis in its visual cortex. Steven Rose repeated these experiments successfully in London at the Imperial College. In Edinburgh William Watson fed salt water to rats and measured an increase in RNA production in the supraoptic nerve cells of those animals.

The term "giant molecule" is a misnomer, as Watson and

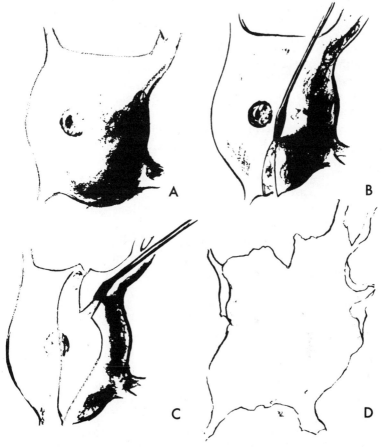

Drawings show Hydén's steps in dissection of individual neurons— (A) whole nerve; (B) initial cut; (C) cut along dendrite; (D) prepared cell membrane.

Crick, the scientists who broke the genetic code, became well aware. They could only infer DNA's structure from shadowy glimpses through the medium of the X-ray diffractometer. Even the neuron, comprising a multitude of molecules, is tiny. It is one thing to theorize that the synthesis of RNA is taking place during the learning process but something else again to prove conclusively that the assumption is correct. Hydén set himself the incredible task of physically weighing and measuring the protein synthesis he believed was taking place within the neurons during animal learning. The precision required can be imagined by remembering that the brain cells involved are only a few thousandths of a centimeter in size and weigh only a few thousandths of a microgram.

Weighing an entire neuron is akin to making physical measurements of a gnat's eyebrow. Hydén's project called for far more spectacular accuracy—he proposed to weigh the change in a neuron caused by learning. Train the gnat and see if his eyebrows gain weight!

Dr. Hydén and his associates laboriously learned over a period of several years how to dissect individual neurons, including the smaller glial cells in the brain. This was done with a tool made from wire only fifteen microns thick. Then a micron knife was used to cut the nucleus from the cell! For some of the grosser operations, Hydén and his workers were able to use micromanipulators, mechanical fingers scaled down by levers to do tiny jobs. But the critical part of the dissecting tasks had to be performed *freehand* by a biologist peering intently into a binocular microscope trained on a bit of tissue barely visible to the eye. Such feats in themselves are a fantastic achievement but are only tiny, incidental steps in Hydén's overall research into whether RNA synthesis is involved in the memory trace.

Hydén knew that although all cells produce RNA, there is a wide variance in the amount produced, ranging from twenty to several thousand micromicrograms per cell. Neurons are great producers of RNA. In goldfish there are "Mauthner" cells that contain an average of ten thousand micromicrograms of RNA. And about eight thousand micromicrograms are in the axon, which in the goldfish is growing constantly. Hydén first investigated stimulated production of RNA in the barracuda. He found that during extended periods of heightened activity, these fish produced a great increase in the RNA content of their neurons.

Dr. Hydén performing freehand dissection of a single neuron under the binocular microscope.

For example, prior to activity there were about 3250 micromicrograms of RNA per neuron. After swimming to exhaustion, the fish produced more than four thousand micromicrograms of RNA. Twenty-two hours later the RNA content had dropped back to normal.

The mere increase in RNA content was dismissed by Hydén as a criterion for the measurement of learning. Not only was the barracuda experiment not a learning process, but increased RNA production has been noted in other cells—the liver, for example. The next experiments were conducted with rabbits and then with rats, more conventional laboratory subjects than barracudas. First Hyden simply rotated the animals on a horizontal disc. A slight increase in RNA was noted. However, when rats were placed on a vertical wheel and rocked back and forth to

Rat learning to climb wire in Hydén's experiments on molecular basis for memory.

induce stress, RNA increased by 20 percent. Thus far the results paralleled those of the barracuda tests—stress produced more RNA in the neurons of test animals. But stress was not a learning process; therefore, Hydén began to refine his measurements.

RNA is made up of four bases—adenine, guanine, cytosine, and uracil, with guanine and cytosine present in greater quantities. Hydén began measuring not just the gross change in RNA but the changes in the amount of the various bases. The task now was to weigh not just the gnat's eyebrow but find the separate weights of its chemical constituents. This required refined laboratory techniques, including electrophoresis, X-ray microspectrography, and analog-digital scanning techniques. These finicky measurements showed no appreciable change in the *kind* of RNA produced in the neurons of test animals subjected to stress.

Now it was time to subject the rats to actual learning. They were not fed for several days and then were placed in a cage with a thin wire leading at a forty-five-degree angle up to a platform containing food. Although the hungry rats had never before balanced on a wire, 90 percent of them were successful in climbing it to reach the food. Learning had obviously taken place.

Analysis of brain RNA in the rats showed about a 10 percent overall increase, not in itself indicative by Hydén's standards. However, although the guanine and cytosine bases remained about the same, the adenine and uracil changed appreciably, the adenine increasing from 21.4 to 24.1 and the uracil down from 20.5 to 18.2. Learning was accompanied by a change in RNA composition. As in the barracuda experiments, tests administered twenty-four hours later showed that base ratios had returned to their prelearning levels.

The neurons analyzed by Hydén in these learning experiments were Deiter's cells taken from the area of the animal's brain that is involved in balance. This area was selected because the learning involved the balancing mechanism. Deiter's cells are also conveniently larger than cortical neurons, and Hydén also pointed out that they should be simpler in anatomy than the more complex cortical neurons. When he was asked whether or not true learning was involved in a simple balancing act, Hydén admitted that investigation of cortical neurons would be a good experiment; but he reminded critics that performing even the simpler Deiter's cell evaluations took several years.

Later Hydén did extend his experiments to more sophisticated learning, including training rats to use the "unpreferred" paw in pressing a lever for food. This is a standard learning task used by psychologists, in contrast to the simple balance task of the wire-

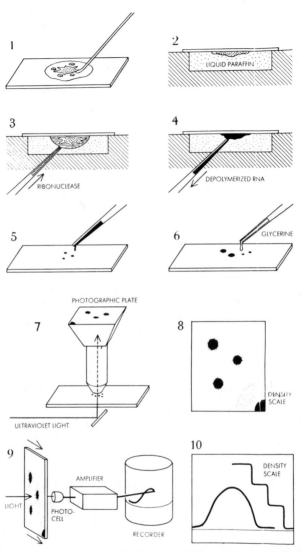

Detailed steps in measurement of RNA in brain cells. Single nerve cell is placed under glass slide (1) Ribonuclease breaks down giant molecules of RNA (3) and this depolymerized RNA is redissolved in glycerine solution (6) Ultraviolet micrograph yields an image of drops (7) and a density scale (8) that is measured by photomultiplier (9).

climbing experiment. Again Hydén found that more RNA was produced and that the base ratio changed as in the earlier tests. In 1968 B. Machlus and J. Gaito of New York University reported evidence of synthesis of RNA in mice involved in learning. Using very sophisticated techniques, including radioactivity tracers, the two men demonstrated that a unique type of RNA was produced in the brains of rats trained for fifteen minutes in an electric shock compartment.

Molecular Mechanics   Hydén has very definite ideas
about what his experiments demonstrate:

> Let us assume that the material background of memory consists of a spatial arrangement of molecules and intramolecular properties in the brain cells. Patterns of electrical currents are assumed to be part of the mechanism of their formation, but not the part which secures the stable, long-lasting memory function, since memory can survive a stoppage of the electrical activity of the brain.
>
> Can we visualize a molecular mechanism for learning and memory in brain cells that is linked to the mechanism for coding of genetic information that we have just discussed? . . .
>
> What happens when an animal is placed in an acute learning situation for which there is no precedence in its life? I would suggest that the time pattern of frequencies set up in the neurons involved leads to a release of repressed regions of chromosomal DNA. This leads to a release of highly specific DNA-copied RNA. In its turn, the RNA synthesis occurring on the demand of the situation gives, as an end product, specific proteins in the neuronal soma. The presence of these proteins, or, at later stages, their rate of production, leads to an activation of the transmitter substance. The next time the same modulated frequencies enter, these specific proteins answer with a rapid reaction, leading to an activation of the transmitter substance. In analogy to the mechanism of an antigen-antibody reaction, the specific proteins react to the same modulated frequencies which first lead to the release of the chromosomal activity, the synthesis of the DNA-dependent RNA, and their own formation.
>
> By such a mechanism there could occur a chemical specification of neurons situated within the phylogenetically given pathways

where the stimulus entered, and also specification of millions of neurons situated outside the first area. . . .

The Sticky State   It is Hydén's contention that the glia, those sticky cells surrounding the neurons, play a much more important part in memory than just providing nourishment to the neurons, as many assume.

> . . . I would like to suggest that, in the learning and memory mechanism, the neuronal glia regulate the induction of RNA synthesis in the neuron, being an integrated part of the memory mechanism, also. . . .
>
> In an acute learning situation, the modulated frequencies set up by the neuron are also transferred to the glia. The glia are characterized by potentials of a 500–1,000-fold longer duration than those recorded from nerve cells. When the neural frequency is changed, a lock-in effect brings the slow frequency of the glia into synchrony, the difference being a multiple. This coupling

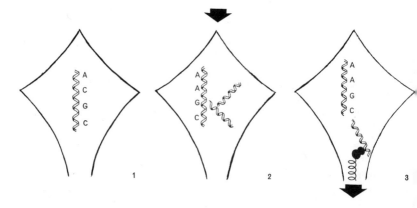

Biochemical theory of memory, proposed by Dr. Hydén, accounts for storage and retrieval of information by protein synthesis. Top, a neuron in which RNA is replicating within the nucleus. Message arriving at the cell (center) causes a modification in the structure of the RNA. This RNA is discharged into the surrounding cytoplasm (bottom) where a memory protein is produced. Memory is recalled by restimulation of the neuron, causing the protein to break down and the neuron to "fire."

of the frequencies of the neuron and the glia forms an information system. The glial ionic equilibrium is disturbed and substrates in the form of nucleotides are transferred from the glia to the neuron to release the repressed chromosome region and induce the necessary enzyme synthesis for the RNA production.

This lock-in mechanism would therefore constitute the information system whereby the specific RNA was synthesized, triggered, or mediated by the glia as a regulator. As was stressed in the discussion earlier, the glia have many features of a feed-back system.

The glia are composed of multiple, thin membranes. Such a composition is well suited for rapid processes, for example, proton transfer.

Both the glia and the neuron constitute a unit. As I see it, that is the functional unit of the nervous system. . . .

Although his experiments have shown only that very simple learning is accompanied by a temporary change in RNA composition and Hydén admits there is no evidence for a stable change in brain RNA through experience, he nevertheless feels that an RNA mechanism may suffice for even the highest type of learning—cognitive acts that lead to insight and creativity.

Hydén points to the obvious advantage that a molecular mechanism would have in storing large amounts of information. Estimating some twenty-five bits of information stored each second for ten hours a day over a ten-year period, he then points out that a tiny amount of RNA could code this data. Others have suggested the same advantage, that a single molecule has the potential capacity for the storage of information contained in a thousand books!

Summing up his theory, Hydén says, "I would favor the view that frequency modulation would lead to synthesis of distinctive RNA molecules and specific end-products, proteins formed through the mediation of this RNA."

Dr. Peter Fong of the Physics Department of Emory University in Atlanta, Georgia, recently advanced an intriguing theory of chemical memory and "playback" reminiscent of Hydén's. According to Fong, who presented a paper on the subject at the spring meeting of the American Physical Society in April, 1969, RNA in the neurons functions something like a tape recorder of information. A nerve pulse of about 120 millivolts impinges on an RNA molecule, imparting an energy of 10^{-13} erg to it. Interestingly, this energy is just equal to that required to "unstack" one of the flat nitrogenous bases that, along with thousands of others, make up the spiral molecule.

An average nerve pulse has a duration of about one millisecond, and, coincidentally, RNA synthesis is believed to proceed at a rate that corresponds exactly to one base formed during each nerve pulse. Because of the ferroelectrical properties of RNA, the unstacked bases would "play back" pulses exactly equivalent to those that unstacked them in the first place. Perhaps the greatest argument against Fong's theory is its marvelous agreement of both pulse strength and duration and RNA synthesis and base dimensions.

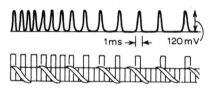

Diagram of Fong theory showing how nerve pulses in brain "unstack" the bases of RNA molecules, analogous to the way in which electrical pulses magnetize tape-recorder tape.

Dr. Samuel Barondes, of Albert Einstein College of Medicine at Yeshiva University in New York, feels that it is likely that memories are deposited by alterations in functional synaptic relations. Barondes has established through laboratory experiments that protein synthesis in the neuron cell body accompanies learning. Furthermore, the protein travels along the axon of the cell to the synapse, where it is thought to facilitate electrochemical connection across that "switch."

It has long been evident that some neuronal interconnections are specified genetically. Experiments like cutting the optic nerve of animals show that the hundreds of thousands of cells involved somehow grew back to the proper mates. This property of specificity is an example of chemical memory—the neurons "smell out" the proper connections for some networks. For some scientists the chemical basis for acquired or experiential memory involves simply an extension of this genetic specificity of the neurons.

Using radioactive tracers, Barondes and his colleagues found that protein synthesized in the neuron cell body was slowly transported along the axon. Although this movement progressed far too slowly to account for short-term memory, Barondes judges that it could occur rapidly enough to set up long-term memory.

Not all researchers are ready to concede that specific memory molecules are produced by learning and that these molecules constitute the memory trace. Fairly typical of the reaction to the more dramatic implications of molecular memory is that of Steven Rose, of Imperial College, London:

> More likely, in my view, is that what occurs when a memory is fixed is something more like what the neurophysiologists have long postulated—a change in the probability of a particular nerve cell firing, caused by alteration in the biochemical state of the cell. Most probably, we should look for changes in the capacity of the synapse to transmit a message to the postsynaptic nerve cell. Such a change might be reflected in an increased size of a particular synapse, or altered quantities of transmitted substance within it, or even a more permeable synaptic membrane.

The "Codons" of Memory However, although caution runs high in many memory camps, there are those who don't flinch at the memory molecule idea. Among these is Frank Rosenblatt of Cornell, whose work with perceptrons we have discussed. Along with his artificial perceptrons, Rosenblatt also experimented with living memory systems and performed on rats many successful transfer experiments, which will be described in another chapter. What he terms as a "most surprising series of experiments" stimulated his thinking on the subject of biochemical memory. The results of this thinking, which he himself characterizes as "science fiction," were presented at the second Computer and Informational Sciences Symposium in 1967.

Rosenblatt considers that long-term memory (the type covered by this theory) involves the preferential gain in stability of

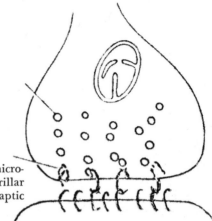

Drawing made from photomicrograph showing "hooklike fibrillar extensions" linking across synaptic cleft.

connections between certain axons and dendrites at their synaptic junctions. Thus "information-carrying molecules" must be able to identify certain pairs of presynaptic and postsynaptic cells so that the proper connections can be made.

Learning, or the acquisition of a memory, triggers a chain of events that results in the establishment or strengthening of proper connections over a period of several hours or days. These synaptic connections are assured by the production of "adhesive molecular complexes," as Rosenblatt calls them. This complex is chemically coded to match up cells.

Rosenblatt envisages far more activity at the synaptic cleft, or space between membranes, than do most other researchers. Although the cleft is generally considered to be a gap, or a liquid-filled area, he points out that intrasynaptic filaments or "neurofibrils" are known to be produced in the cell endbulbs. These sizable protein structures tumble into the cleft, somewhat like logs into a stream, and Rosenblatt pictures them as joining together to form bridges across the cleft. At first this was pure theory on his part, but he learned later that electron microscopes pictured neurofibrils coming from both endbulbs and joining in "hooklike junctions" within the cleft! As further proof of this physical connection between the endbulbs, Rosenblatt points to the fact that in centrifugation processes involving neurons, the tearing away of a presynaptic endbulb also involves the carrying along of some postsynaptic membrane. This would seem to indicate a physical connection across the cleft.

The manner in which the neurofibrils link to form bridges across the cleft is the heart of Rosenblatt's memory molecule theory. He sees the neurofibrils as chemically coded so that they accept certain strings of amino acids that are also produced in the endbulbs and that are ejected into the synaptic cleft. Rosenblatt names these neurofibrils "codons" after the similar entities involved in the DNA molecule of the gene. The codons are assembled in groups to form the proper code for identification of cells.

Rosenblatt sees a competitive process continually prevailing at synaptic sites, with cell endings probing for new contacts. Needed are "adhesive complexes" at the proper junctions of cells, and the neurofibrils and codons provide these adhesions or sticky connections. As in the gene, there are sites on the neurofibril that

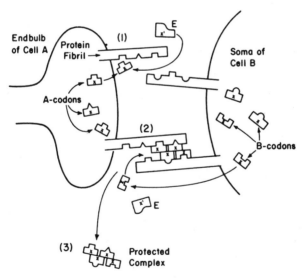

Rosenblatt's proposed molecular memory mechanism. Because of proper molecular coding, neurofibrils link together to match templates of fibrils. Codons of memory perform functions similar to those involved in genetic mechanism.

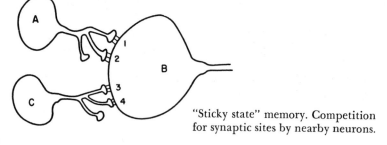

"Sticky state" memory. Competition for synaptic sites by nearby neurons.

will receive certain codons. These link up as shown in the drawing; and where two neurofibrils and codons touch, a further link is effected. At synapses not intended to be linked, the proper codons are not formed and those that are formed are quickly destroyed by enzymes in the cleft.

Rosenblatt's model suggests a memory molecule that is analogous to the DNA gene molecule and whose codons form the "memory" of cell structure. He extends the idea to include competing nerve endings being favored by memory molecules over contacts with adjacent cells and terms this memory theory "the survival of the stickiest." His calculations show that codons of seven or eight amino acid residues (polypeptides) would yield sufficient combinations to differentiate all the synapses of the human brain. The molecular weight of the codon complexes would be 5600. Interestingly, the actual molecular weights of brain extracts thought to be memory transfer agents is about 5000.

Although Rosenblatt's memory molecule theory is not as rigorous a concept as that of Hydén, Rosenblatt's chemical memory envisages such an entity being fed through the brain over a period of time and being so carefully coded that it lodges only where it is intended to. The theory is a compromise, a joining together and synthesis of the "connectionist" theory and the "molecular" theory.

More Tests   The battle of memory still rages, but the molecular or biochemical theory has already made revolutionary changes in thinking and research in this field. In this chapter we have discussed one experimental method for investigating the theory—teaching an animal subject and then measuring the chemical changes that take place in its neurons. There are other methods currently being used. In one the chemistry of the brain is tampered with by injecting chemicals and then measuring the effects of this interference on the ability to learn. The most intriguing experiment involves an actual transfer of learning to untrained animals by injecting them with extracts from trained animals. We shall look at these two methods in the next two chapters.

Chapter Eleven

DRUGS AND MEMORY

The brain is basically a chemical machine, composed of living cells. The lowliest cells are remarkable bits of protoplasm. Most cells carry out the complex business of converting nutrients to energy, but some have even more specialized tasks. For instance, many organs and glands of the body secrete chemical compounds known as hormones. The pancreas and its production of insulin is an example. The pituitary secretes a number of vital hormones, including ACTH, which in turn activates the adrenal cortex to produce cortisone and other compounds. Gonadotrophins stimulate the ovaries or the testes to produce progesterone or testosterone. Thyrotropin goes to the thyroid and causes the production of thyroxin; somatotropin regulates bone growth.

Neurons are the most sophisticated, most specialized, of all cells. One writer has described this sophistication in the following manner. Most living cells are undifferentiated, like the individual bulbs in a bank of lights illuminating a stadium. If one "goes out," no great harm is done and perhaps the loss will not even be noticed. Brain cells, however, are specialized components, like the different tubes in a TV set. If one TV tube fails, the whole picture may go dark. Although brain cells are basically similar to cells in other parts of the body, they differ importantly in specific details, just as the tubes in a TV set are diffentiated in order to perform their specialized functions.

In an earlier chapter we examined the activity of the synapse, or "firing switch" in the neuron. It is known that electrical activity in the neuron causes the production of a chemical substance in the axon that is then diffused across the synaptic cleft to the receptor. Among these transmitted chemical compounds are the amines (organic derivatives of ammonia) epinephrine, norepinephrine, acetylcholine, serotonin, and dopamine. Amines from other parts of the body are blocked by the "blood brain" barrier from entering the brain. The brain uses only its own supply, the endogenous amines. Exogenous amines are those injected into the brain from outside.

Electrical stimulation of a neuron, then, results in the flow of a neurohormone across the synaptic cleft, at which point this neurohormone excites or inhibits the output signal. The excitation can be a memory, an emotion, a control movement, and so on. Now let's look at the effect of drugs—chemicals administered from without—on the neuron.

History of Mind Drugs
For thousands of years men have known in a vague and unscientific way that chemical compounds eaten or otherwise ingested have a dramatic and often drastic mental effect. The history of such drugs—natural and manmade—is long, colorful, and sometimes horrific.

Animals occasionally eat plants that have an effect on their minds. Locoweed is an example. Perhaps it is only because animals are incapable of doing so that they do not seek out more refined stimulants or depressants for their minds; domesticated animals, given the opportunity, sometimes become habitual users of alcohol. Man's mind is much advanced over the minds of lesser beings and although his use of psychic drugs must have begun accidentally, he subsequently began actively to seek out chemical compounds that produced pleasant sensations. The use of mind-changing drugs has been consciously practiced for thousands of years. Mandrake root, night-shade, henbane, and belladonna are familiar. These drugs contain the narcotic alkaloids scopolamine, hyoscyamine, atropine, and polandrene.

The Pythian priestesses at Delphos used narcotic plant drugs to stimulate their oracular predictions. The Greeks also cultivated a state of mind called *ataraxia,* a condition of pleasurable well-being. Simply by exercising tremendous willpower, the reli-

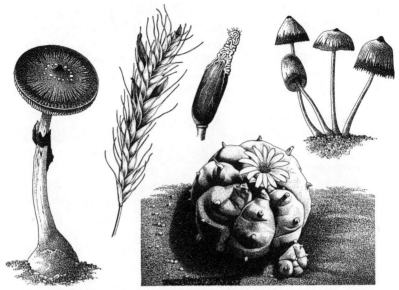

Natural sources of the main hallucinogens. Psilocybin comes from the mushrooms *Stropharia cubensis* and *Psilocybe mexicana* (left and top right). LSD is synthesized from ergot, a fungus that grows on grains; the two center drawings show ergot-infested rye seed and detail of fungus. Mescaline comes from peyote cactus *Lophophora williamsii* (bottom right).

gious or the philosophic could achieve a euphoric state, but shortcuts, such as the legendary Vedic substance known as *soma,* were sometimes taken. There was *nepenthe,* of which Homer and other poets, including John Keats, have sung in grateful praise; the Greeks also had *ambrosia,* the fruit of the gods. The Aztecs ate the sacred *peyotl* and the Incas found psychic blessing in *coca.* The Indians of Asia used *charas,* a derivative of the hemp plant, as a mind drug. Tobacco was adopted for its euphoric effect, which was far milder than that of other mind drugs. Tobacco does, indeed, have an effect on the mind, slight as that effect may be.

Opium became a popular mind-changing drug, and users ranging from Chinese coolies to literary greats succumbed to its appeal. Alcohol, marijuana, and many other substances became popular, too. Euphoria was euphoria, whether it came from living the good life, from contemplating one's navel with proper introspection, or from imbibing, inhaling, or chewing some medication for the mind. At times men destroyed their own minds, burning them out with the dangerous chemicals. At other times tragic accidents drove whole villages mad as a result of using moldy rye flour. This was *ergot,* which was later to lead to the most potent of the psychodrugs.

Barbiturates were developed to yield the ultimate in forgetfulness. Painkillers like morphine and cocaine were greatly misused for purposes other than the relief of pain. Psychiatrists became interested in drugs—Freud made the mistake of recommending to a friend that he shake the morphine habit by switching to cocaine.

Humphrey Davy tested "laughing gas" on himself and others and found that it affected recollections and memory, leading to "stream of consciousness" thoughts that were startling. Davy described it this way: "I gradually began to lose the perception of external things, and a *vivid and intense recollection* of some former experiences passed through my mind. . . ."

Dr. Peter Roget, before he wrote his famous thesaurus, was another subject for the nitrous oxide tests. Interestingly, he noted:

> My ideas succeeded one another with extreme rapidity, thoughts rushed like a torrent through my mind, *as if their velocity had been suddenly accelerated by the bursting of a barrier which had before retained them in their natural and equable course.*

In both cases the italics have been added to underscore the idea that both intensity and speed of recollection were increased by the drug.

Another who used nitrous oxide and noted its effects was the psychologist William James. There have been many books on mind-changing chemicals, ranging from horror-filled tales of hashish-eaters to the delightful *Alice in Wonderland,* surely a psychedelic fable if ever there was one. Lewis Lewin was a pioneer clinical chronicler of what he called "Phantastica," the mind-changing drugs. This was in 1928, and the new, scientific age of psychopharmacology was just beginning. Amphetamine was developed in the early 1930s. Here was a drug that heightened perception, pepped up the user instead of tranquilizing him.

Present-day "psychedelic" (mind-*opening* or mind-*erasing?*) drugs had their natural beginnings in the *peyotl* of the Aztecs and the *peyote* of American Indians. These "buttons" from a small cactus, when eaten, result in delightful sensations, heightened perception, and visions of great beauty. Among the better-known users were Havelock Ellis, writer on sexual mores, and Aldous Huxley, pessimistic predicter of the future. Huxley experimented with peyote, considering it similar to the *soma* of his *Brave New World*.

In 1943 Swiss researcher Albert Hoffman discovered that laboratory-produced LSD, a derivative of ergot, the rye mold that had terrorized French peasants centuries earlier, caused fantastic hallucinations. Working in his laboratory in Basel with a lysergic acid compound derived from ergot, Hoffman accidentally ingested some of the stuff. Shortly he felt ill and went home and to bed. His illness was the strangest he had ever encountered:

> . . . a not unpleasant state of drunkenness which was characterized by an extremely stimulating fantasy. When I closed my eyes (the daylight was most unpleasant to me) I experienced fantastic images of an extraordinary plasticity. They were associated with an intense kaleidoscopic play of colors. . . .

He had taken the first LSD trip. Not since Humphrey Davy's nitrous oxide in 1799 had man produced such a synthetic hallucinogen in a laboratory. Here was a far more potent mind drug than raw peyote or even its derivative, mescaline. A few millionths of a gram of LSD, hardly visible, caused Hoffman to have such severe hallucinations that he knew he had stumbled onto something potent. Twenty-five years later the "acid head" has testified to the correctness of Hoffman's analysis. LSD-25, short for d-lysergic acid diethylamide tartrate, produces a psychedelic world of visions for its users. It also drives some out of their minds, and a few investigators suspect that it causes women users to give birth to genetically flawed children.

Insulin makes up for deficiencies in the pancreas; iodine injected artificially aids a lagging thyroid. Injections of sex hormones balance the makeup of humans with problems of this nature. Thalidomide drastically affects the genetic mechanism. And for thousands of years there has been evidence that "exogenous amines" affect man's brain in much the same manner as chemicals cause changes in other organs.

The drugging of the mind first took place as addiction, by accident, or as a side effect. What happens when we scientifically inject the proper chemicals from outside instead of relying on the chemicals that the brain itself normally produces? We have learned accidentally and incidentally that drugs can kill brain cells just as they kill other cells. Short of that, drugs can also induce madness, sleep, fantastic visions—all the sensations and emotions in spades. Drugs can cause insanity and destroy memory. Can they *enhance* memory and cure insanity, too? Shortly after the turn of the century, scientists began serious investigation into the effects of drugs on man's mind.

The Chemical Stimulation of Memory   We have seen that Karl Lashley was for a long time an advocate of the "reverberation" theory of memory; he felt that the phenomenon was electrical in nature and composed of dynamic currents circling through neuron networks of the brain. However, he could never locate such sites and finally wrote in good-humored despair that "learning just is not possible." This statement seemed particularly true with respect to learning about memory, but Lashley persevered. In 1916 he investigated the effects of chemicals injected into the brains of mice on their ability to learn. He reported that strychnine increased their maze-learning performance, an indication that their memories were enhanced by the drug.

About this time the chemical theory of memory received another strong boost as the result of research conducted in Europe. Sir Henry Dale was an English biologist whose studies included work with the fungus ergot, the stuff that drove villagers mad. From ergot Dale isolated the chemical compound acetylcholine in the second decade of this century.

In the meantime, the German physiologist Otto Loewi, whom Dale had met while both were studying under the English physiologist Henry Starling at University College in London, was busy. Starling was the discoverer and namer of hormones. His pupil Loewi went on to prove (with help from dreams, as we have seen), in studies with a frog's heart, that when a nerve is stimulated electrically it produces a chemical substance. He extracted some of this substance and used it, without the intervention of nerve activity, to stimulate another heart. When Dale heard of Loewi's proof that nerve action was electrochemical, he showed that the chemical produced was the acetylcholine he had found in ergot! Acetylcholine is present in the brain as well as in the heart; therefore, it was small wonder that ergot affected the mind. The two men were awarded a Nobel Prize in 1936 for their work.

At about the same time, psychiatrists in America were making another exciting find. As with many great scientific discoveries, narcosynthesis came about quite by accident. In 1916 Arthur S. Loevenhart at the University of Wisconsin was testing narcotic drugs to determine their effects as respiratory stimulants. He found that the chemicals also had a profound effect on the *minds* of mental patients, greatly relaxing them and making them more able to recall and discuss past experiences. By the 1930s "narco-analysis," the use of so-called truth drugs in analysis, was a common psychiatric method.

Sodium amytal and Sodium Pentothal, both synthetics, later emerged as the most efficacious of the "truth drugs" when the natural drug scopolamine proved too toxic. These drugs are not really truth serums, despite Hollywood movies whose climaxes hinged on a dramatic use of the new drugs. However, it was obvious that the drugs were doing *something* to the chemistry of the brain and bringing about remarkable changes as a result. Most interestingly, these mind-affecting drugs bore a notable resemblance in molecular structure to hormones produced naturally in the brain.

That the brain's operation was electrochemical had been firmly established for some time. However, the actual mechanism of memory was hardly better understood than when Lashley wrote that learning just wasn't possible. Narcoanalysis seemed to bring back vivid memory details, but so did hypnosis. Some psychiatrists said that truth drugs merely put the subject in the proper mood for suggestion by his analyst. Despite these criticisms, however, there was growing evidence that memory traces were perhaps physicochemical changes wrought in neurons by experience.

Lashley had showed that strychnine seemed to enhance maze learning in mice. So did curare, amphetamine, and nicotine. Later experiments added picrotoxin to the growing list of chemicals. Renewed work with strychnine and picrotoxin indicated that strychnine blocked *post*synaptic inhibitory pathways, whereas picrotoxin blocked *pre*synaptic inhibition. It would have been more understandable if the injected chemicals had *harmed* memory in the subject animals, because both chemicals are toxic even in fairly small doses! A search was made for milder chemicals that would improve memory, and soon the new drug pentylenetetrazol (trade name Metrazol) was claimed to speed learning in mice. Metrazol apparently did so not by blocking synaptic inhibition but by decreasing the recovery time of neurons following excitation. The refractory or waiting period between firings of the neuron was a well-known phenomenon; now a drug existed that shortened this time between transmission of synaptic signals.

"Memory drugs" quickly became widely used—and highly controversial—in laboratory experiments across the country. An example is the drug Cylert. The best-known memory drug to date, Cylert is Abbott Laboratories' trade name for the compound magnesium pemoline. This compound was used for some time in Europe as a stimulant of the central nervous system before American memory researchers picked it up. Using it on mice, Alvin J. Glasky of Abbott and Lionel N. Simon of Illinois State Pediatric Institute demonstrated that Cylert increased the rate of production of the protein molecule RNA. RNA is ribonucleic acid, thought by some to be associated with memory formation. Magnesium pemoline, "2-imino-5-phenyl-4-oxazolidi-none and magnesium hydroxide," requires a good memory just to remember its name.

N. Plotnikoff of Abbott also tested the drug on mice and claimed that it enhanced the "acquisition and retention of a conditioned avoidance response in rats." Rats injected with magnesium pemoline were said to learn within two or three trials, whereas control rats injected with a saline solution required seven trials.

The name *Cylert* implies mental alertness, and the drug has enjoyed wide publicity, both scientifically and in the popular press. However, almost as soon as Glasky and Plotnikoff had announced their startling findings that learning in mice was speeded several times by the drug, other researchers began disagreeing. In fact, other scientists at Abbott refuted what their colleagues had claimed.

The controversial experience with Cylert, incidentally, paralleled almost exactly that which earlier researchers had with the drug called glutamic acid. In the 1940s studies of the effects of glutamic acid on the memory of rats were made. The journal *Science* in 1944 described experiments that seemed to show that the drug not only speeded the learning process in white rats but even made them capable of solving problems too complex for rats not given glutamic acid.

Other researchers gave the drug to nine youngsters whose IQs had previously been tested. After six months of receiving glutamic acid dosage, the children were retested and all showed some increase in intelligence. Encouraged, the scientists broadened the scope of the experiment by increasing the number of children tested to sixty-nine. Tested six months later, this group showed an average increase in IQ of eight points. It was found that children who were seriously retarded mentally showed the greatest increase in IQ.

Dramatic as these experiments were, little came of them and interest in them waned. Perhaps there was more optimism than accuracy, and as noted in the chapter on intelligence, no run developed on glutamic acid at the corner drugstore. It was reported in 1966 that new and well-controlled studies showed no improvement in the subjects' intelligence.

The Inhibition of Memory   Poisonous chemical compounds had first been used to enhance remembering. Now some researchers went full circle and began to inject antibiotics to *curb* memory. The theory behind this approach was that antibiotics slowed the rate of protein formation in the brain and would thus hamper learning—if protein was indeed involved in the learning process. Early experiments included those of C. Wesley Dingman II and M. B. Sporn of the National Institute of Health; these men injected 8-azaguanine (similar to guanine, which is one of the amines making up DNA in living things) into mice. Other researchers used puromycin in similar experiments that seemed to indicate that learning did indeed suffer when an antibiotic was injected.

Puromycin experiments on goldfish learning is an example. Choosing the goldfish because it was readily available in the large numbers necessary for valid statistical tests and also small enough not to require much room, researchers at the University of Michigan conducted learning experiments using puromycin as the memory-inhibiting drug. With a "shuttle box" and flashing lights, Dr. Bernard Agranoff trained goldfish to respond to light by swimming to the opposite end of the water-filled box. Some goldfish were given no drug injections; others were injected with puromycin. Dr. Agranoff pointed out that whereas chemicals such as strychnine and cyanide are not only drastic but also general in their effects on the brain cells, antibiotics are highly selective. Some block only one step in cellular metabolism. Puromycin, for example, halts the growth of the RNA molecule in the ribosome of the cell.

As a result of the tests, the workers at Michigan concluded that goldfish injected with puromycin suffered a loss of memory if the antibiotic was injected within an hour following training. Immediate injection resulted in complete elimination of the memory; the longer the period of time before injection, the less the memory loss. After one hour, puromycin had no effect. The compounds acetoxycycloheximide and actinomycin were also used with similar results.

Even the memory-inhibition experiments were controversial, however. As with the memory-enhancement experiments, some researchers reported a failure to achieve the reported inhibitory results. Finally, some advocates of antibiotic inhibition admitted that their results were inconclusive and suggested that perhaps the memory loss was due to "occult seizures" caused by the drug, rather than to any effect on the actual formation of memory. They were in the embarrassing position of the legendary scientist who cut off the legs of trained fleas and announced that this affected their hearing: they no longer stood up on command.

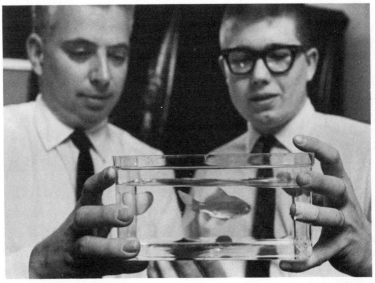

An absent-minded goldfish, being shown to lab assistant Paul Klinger by Dr. Bernard Agranoff (left), professor of biochemistry, is one of a number that are helping science understand the complicated memory process. Dr. Agranoff found that goldfish that had been trained to jump a hurdle in the tank forgot their training when he introduced drugs that blocked the manufacture of protein. The correlation is not yet definite.

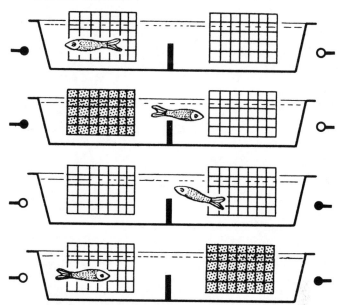

Training goldfish to respond to light. End of tank where fish is swimming is lighted for twenty seconds, and then a shock is given fish through grid shown in drawing. Fish swims to unlighted end of tank to avoid shock. After a few trials, the fish learns to swim to dark end of tank before the shock comes and is then conditioned to the light signal.

The Memory Pill   If chemicals can affect memory in animals, can they similarly affect human memory? Researchers moved into this field, using not cyanide or strychnine, understandably, but such drugs as thiopental. This sedating agent was found to cause a loss of memory of material learned while the subject was under sedation, with a correlation between memory loss and the amount of chemical in the bloodstream at the time of the learning trials. Although learning under sedation would appear to be difficult, researchers demonstrated that the subjects could recall material they had learned while under sedation.

D. Ewen Cameron, then a member of the psychiatry department at McGill University, had been experimenting with ad-

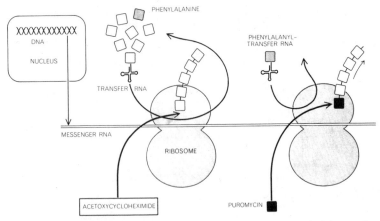

Protein-blocking agents can interrupt the formation of molecules at the ribosome, where the amino acid units of protein are linked according to instructions embodied in messenger RNA. One agent, acetoxycycloheximide, interferes with the bonding mechanism that links amino acids brought to the ribosome by transfer RNA. Puromycin, another agent, resembles the combination of transfer RNA and the amino acid phenylalanine. Thus it is taken into chain and prematurely halts its growth.

ministering RNA to patients plagued with memory problems. Using yeast RNA, Cameron claimed some beneficial results and hoped to be able to get human RNA to give his patients. In 1964, Cameron moved from Canada to Albany, New York, to direct the Veterans Administration Hospital Psychiatry and Aging Research Laboratories. He was interested in the drug magnesium pemoline, which stimulates production of RNA, and began using it with mental patients in 1966. With mice, Cylert had seemed to show a learning rate several times faster than normal. Results with human patients were not so dramatic, but Cameron felt that the drug helped some of them. He began by injecting patients who had suffered a crippling loss of memory, usually connected with old age, but later extended the tests to "essentially normal" men and women. Dr. Cameron died in 1967 and his work with memory drugs has not been continued at Albany.

Memory researchers now claimed to have demonstrated the enhancement of memory by some chemicals and its inhibition by others. However, other researchers continued to report, with equally impressive statistical documentation, that they could not repeat these experiments. In fact, some claimed that their human subjects performed better in learning tests when they were on the placebos, or pink pills, given to the control groups than they did on Cylert.

Part of the confusion arose from the fact that there are two processes under consideration. Dr. Cameron was concerned with restoring the *already established memories* of aging or ill patients. Other researchers were attempting to show improved learning. The first process simply facilitated the "playback" of a memory, a matter of oiling existing switches so that they could produce the information desired. The second process involved the *formation of the memory itself,* the creation of the engram.

It is obvious that the "memory pill" is not yet ready to take its place with all the other pills promoted by science. However, the stakes are high enough to justify all continued efforts to find a

Dr. D. Ewen Cameron, who reported improvement in the memories of his patients when he gave them RNA.

drug that improves memory. Part of that effort is careful scrutiny by the neuropharmacologist and the neurochemist of the chemistry of the synaptic mechanism.

Neuronal Chemistry If chemicals are indeed involved in memory, what mechanisms are responsible for the phenomenon? The nerve impulse itself does not jump across the synapse when it reaches the axon terminal—instead, it causes a chemical, acetylcholine, for example, to be released. This "transmitter" substance rapidly diffuses and excites the postsynaptic region and then is immediately destroyed by an enzyme in order to prevent its continued action. Acetylcholine, for example, is destroyed by the choline esterase.

A variety of chemicals are secreted and stored in the brain. For instance, noradrenaline concentrations are highest in the hypothalamus and in the area postrema. Serotonin predominates in the limbic system. There are also structural and chemical differences among the cells of various portions of the brain as evidenced by their selective response to drugs. Researchers have found some specific and selective affinity of a direct or indirect chemical nature between injected toxins and the chemical organization of that part of the brain injured or destroyed by the toxin. For example, injections of the 8-aminoquinolines in monkey brains show great specificity in the structural changes they cause. So do injections of arsenical compounds.

Basically, two things can be done with a switch, regardless of what kind of switch it is. It can be closed so that it transmits a signal, or it can be opened so that no signal is sent. Two kinds of drugs would seem to be in order: excitatory and inhibitory agents, or put another way, energizing drugs and tranquilizing drugs.

Even in ancient times it was evident that there were two kinds of mind-changers. One was the drink of forgetfulness, a primitive equivalent of the businessman's evening martini or two. The other was the "delight giver" or bringer of pleasant and strangely beautiful visions unseeable in any other way.

F. M. Berger lists five categories of drugs that affect the brain:

sedative-hypnotics, tranquilizers, stimulants, narcotics, and hallucinogenics. Aside from the hallucinogenics, there are two major kinds of psychodrugs—the tranquilizers and the energizers. Reserpine is one of the tranquilizers, and one theory is that it reduces the supply of amines in the neuron and thus makes the synapse less active. On the other hand, imipramine, an antidepressant or energizer, produces a higher concentration of active neurohumoral transmitter substances and makes the synapse more active. A tranquilizing drug generally inhibits the activity of brain cells, whereas an energizer or pep pill stimulates that activity. For example, the time distortion caused in some users' minds by LSD involves memory, but in a different way than a simple recall of past occurrences. The basic excitation-inhibition ability of mind-changing drugs may explain the phenomenon of time distortion through the speeding up or slowing down of synaptic transmission.

The Validity of Memory Concepts   The idea of excitors and inhibitors, although convenient, is not sufficient to explain all the complexities of memory. A variation from the concept of a simple switch that is either off or on lies in the use of antibiotics (which compounds, by the way, are not included in the list of the five brain-affecting drugs) to inhibit protein formation. Even with the obvious shortcomings of the concept, it still remains a useful tool for study and experiment with drugs and memory, much as the idea of the human brain as a collection of on-off switches like those of the computer has validity in certain studies.

Seymour S. Kety, an official of the National Institute of Health, suggests that the neurohormones or amines are linked with the emotions. As we have seen, these amines are concentrated in the limbic system of the brain. Part of the limbic system, the hippocampus, is important in the establishment of memories. Kety says that the amines may be a "setting agent" for the protein "solder" of memory, and he backs up his hypothesis by stating that most meaningful learning is accompanied by emotion.

There are two obvious methods of studying the effects of chemicals in the brain. One, which we have discussed at some length, is to inject drugs into the brain and to observe the results. The other method, which goes at the problem from the opposite direction, is to change the subject's environment and then to examine the chemicals produced in the cells of his body. Such an approach is very difficult to carry out, but some interesting beginnings have been made. Tests of the urine of ice hockey players following games show that those who played produced several times the normal amount of the amine norepinephrine, whereas those who were benched produced more than normal amounts of epinephrine. Thus anxiety-producing situations seem to result in the production of epinephrine, and activity, or "fight," situations yield norepinephrine.

Motivation for Memory Drugs   The news media have given two distinct and diametrically opposed reactions to the notion of memory drugs, much as opposite results have been reported in the scientific journals. In flashy headlines and in magazine articles like "The Pill That Helps You Remember," the popular press has hailed the possibility of memory improvement that is washed down with a swallow of water. Such blue-sky journalism is inevitable, and perhaps even helpful, although it was bound to provoke reactions like the following from *New Scientist:*

> Memory, in the popular mind, is equated with knowledge and the newspapers have never, therefore, been without advertisements for Pelmanism, applied mnemonics, and other variants of You, too, can have a Memory like Mine. The forgetful masses are waiting with ready money for a pill which, without hirsute side-effects, will endow its swallower with total recall. Such a market cannot remain unexploited once a basic product is available and, one inevitable day, mass-produced Cylert, priced within the reach of every pocket, will make walking encyclopedias of us all.
>
> No more will anyone have to look up Hansard to recall exactly what Mr. Harold Wilson said in 1961 about financial policies of Mr. Selwyn Lloyd. We shall all of us be quiz-kings, our minds chock-full of instant, useless facts, and the BBC contest for the

Brain of Britain will become a battle of endurance rather than of erudition. Elephants will slink shamefaced from human paths, feeling by comparison like hidebound, mental sieves. Names will spring to mind at first glimpse of faces, Mr. What's-his-name will vanish from the face of the Earth, and the ubiquitous how-d'you-do and whatchemacallit will disappear from our vocabularies. Diary manufacturers will go on to short time, umbrellas will no longer inhabit lost property offices, and St. Antony will be hard up for business. Wives will have to seek fresh grounds for husband-denigration when all spouses have computer memories and arrive home regularly flower-laden on all birthdays and wedding anniversaries. And humorous writers will sadly lose their oldest scientific friend, the amnesiac boffin, the absent-minded professor.

Such tongue-in-cheek jibes—or even more scholarly rebukes in the learned journals—hardly divert the memory researchers from their task. Indeed, while the controversy raged as to whether or not memory could be enhanced, a dedicated group of scientists provoked even more controversial debate by "proving" that learning could be transferred. Not only was there a memory pill, they seemed to be saying, there was also a "smart pill" that could put a chunk of knowledge into a brain that did not previously have that particular chunk. In addition, this learning transfer seemed entirely chemical, instead of being mastered the hard way. In the next chapter we will look into this amazing prospect.

Chapter Twelve

THE TRANSFER OF LEARNING

> I was at the Mathematical School, where the Master taught his Pupils after a Method scarce imaginable to us in *Europe*. The Proposition and Demonstration were fairly written on a thin Wafer, with Ink composed of Cephalick Tincture. This the Student was to swallow upon a fasting stomach, and for three Days following eat nothing but Bread and Water. As the Wafer digested, the Tincture mounted to his Brain, bearing the Proposition along with it. . . .
>
> Jonathan Swift, *Gulliver's Travels*

We come now to the most provocative experiments yet conducted with memory—the "most surprising series of experiments" to which Frank Rosenblatt referred in describing memory transfer. Within the past few years in the laboratories of several countries it has been demonstrated to the satisfaction of most experts in the field that with "Cephalick Tinctures" learning *is* apparently transferred chemically. The fact that this is a more rudimentary form of memory than Swift's "Proposition and Demonstration" does not greatly lessen the significance of the experiments. Here is a facet of the biochemical revolution that is perhaps as important to man's future as the discovery of the DNA molecule of the gene. Because it involves RNA, and is in some ways similar to genetic coding, memory transfer, like the creation of artificial life, is an exciting—and frightening—possibility for the future.

Learning is big business. Each year in the United States the various levels of government spend more than $50 billion to teach their citizens; industry spends perhaps another $20 billion to educate its employees. To survive we must learn, and early in life we begin to soak up a variety of knowledge. We attend school for many years, and informal learning goes on after we have ceased our formal education. John Dewey was an advocate of lifelong learning; had he not popularized this concept someone else surely would have. We learn because our minds are geared for learning.

Traditionally we "con by rote"; in other words, we drill knowledge into our memories by constant repetition. This was the method used by Ebbinghaus to learn strings of nonsense syllables. In many cases our schools still teach by this method. We commit information to memory by impressing it on our neurons, synapses, or whatever part of the brain it is that stores such bits of data. Is there some easier way, some shortcut for getting information into the brain? Can learning be transferred chemically?

We can take a spring-powered toy car and push it backward until it has stored up enough energy to go forward about the same distance. Let's stretch a point and call this energy *knowledge*. By pushing the car we have "trained" it to roll along the ground. There is a simpler way we can train the car to do the same thing—we can wind up the spring with a key. The unwinding spring results in the same action that was caused by pushing the car.

Consider another analogy. A phonograph record has a spirally grooved "memory trace" cut into it that enables it to play certain sounds. The trace can be cut into the record by a process like that of rolling the toy car backward. Or it can be impressed by a mass-production technique. In either case, the same information is imparted to the record. The record has acquired a memory, not by going through the experience of hearing a song but by being instantaneously imprinted.

In the last chapter we considered the use of drugs and other means to enhance learning. Surely an elixir that aids in the assimilation of information would be a highly marketable beverage. Even more desirable would be *bottled knowledge* itself, a liquid swimming with facts and figures that would go straight to one's head. Mythology and legend tell of streams that run with knowledge "whereat even a dunce might become learned as he quaffed his fill." We traditionally "thirst" for knowledge, after all.

We infer that in learning, some change takes place in the brain. Can we effect this change by more direct means than the laborious repetition that slowly builds up a memory trace? Surprisingly, some scientists think that we can. Even more surprisingly, they seem to have demonstrated this ability by grinding up educated flatworms and feeding the mixture of worm and learning to ignorant flatworms. The worms fed on this heady diet seemingly acquire the learning of their sacrificed mentors!

It has been jokingly suggested that old professors could be ground up into instant learning, consumed by their pupils, and thus impart knowledge in a most personal way. The memory experts have not yet got around to putting worn-out professors in the meat grinder to make cram-course hamburgers for undergraduates. But many such learning transfer experiments have been conducted with animals.

Dugesia dorotocephala, a flatworm, would not seem to be a particularly distinguished candidate for higher education. This planarian lives under rocks in stagnant polluted water. Less than an inch long, it has a distinctive flattened shape that gives it its name. Dugesia is a very primitive form of life but is advanced enough to be a subject for the simple learning tasks. The flatworm has a rudimentary brain plus sensors and muscles that generate and respond to brain signals. The flatworm has one of the lowliest intellects in the world, but it is still sufficient to test the learning transfer theory.

Just as Pavlov trained dogs to salivate on receiving a neutral stimulus, experimenters can train the flatworm to respond to stimuli. For example, at the same time that a light bulb is flashed on over the flatworm, it receives a mild electric shock. This shock causes a contraction of the flatworm's body. Now, the contraction in itself is a reflex action and not a learned response—yet. But after two hundred or so combined light flashes and electric proddings, the flatworm behaves the way that Pavlov's dogs did. When the light flashes, the flatworm contracts his body, even without the assistance of the electric shock. It is somewhat as if we experienced rain every Thursday for years and gradually got into the habit of putting on our raincoats just because it was a certain day of the week instead of because it was wet outside.

In 1953 a twenty-eight-year-old psychologist named James V. McConnell began to conduct learning studies using planaria as subjects. Psychologist D. O. Hebb had theorized that learning involved changes at the synapses of neurons; thus the planarian, the simplest animal equipped with a brain and synapses, should be the lowest creature capable of learning. Some research had already been done in this regard.

A Dutch biologist named P. van Oye had published a paper in 1920 describing his work on learning in planaria. At the University of Texas, McConnell and a colleague named Robert Thompson were unaware of the van Oye experiments, but they had read the papers of American psychologist H. B. Hovey. Hovey reported in 1929 that he had been able to "extinguish" the response to light stimuli of a marine flatworm called Leptoplana. He did this by tapping the animal each time it responded normally to the light. This training was similar to Pavlov's famous experiments with dogs that were conditioned to salivate at the ringing of a bell. A few years after Hovey's work two German scientists attempted more sophisticated classical conditioning with planaria.

Noting a lack of "control groups" of flatworms in the previous studies, McConnell and Thompson devised more sophisticated tests. Two control groups were used, in fact. In conditioning rats, psychologists use the familiar grid floor in cages and attach wires to the grid so that they can administer light shocks to the animals at the desired time. The planarian is more at home in water so the researchers devised a new shock system. Electrodes were inserted in each end of a water-filled trough, which made it possible to pass a weak current through the water.

Basically, the experiments were similar to those of Hovey and others. Lights were turned on as the planarian swam in its trough, and simultaneously a shock was given. The electric shock was similar to the meat that Pavlov gave his dogs—it always induced a response, in this case a vigorous contraction of the planarian's body. With no conditioning, the worm responded to the light flash with contractions only 25 percent of the time. After 150 trials, however, the response to light increased to 50 percent.

The control groups were given either light alone or shock alone; the two stimuli were never paired. These control groups showed a *decrease* in contraction response to light alone as a result of their training. Comparing the performance of the groups, McConnell and Thompson felt they had demonstrated classical conditioning in the planarian, although McConnell later said he would leave to other psychologists the interpretation of the behavioral changes he wrought in the flatworms—whether

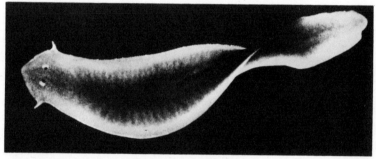

Flatworm, or planarian, used in remarkable memory transfer experiments by Dr. James V. McConnell and others.

these changes constituted true classical conditioning or "conditioned sensitization." He and Thompson published their first paper in 1955. Soon afterward McConnell went to the University of Michigan, where he continued his experiments with flatworms.

With Allan Jacobson and Daniel Kimble, McConnell now conducted more sophisticated experiments in which he was able to train flatworms to the point where they responded to light stimuli more than 90 percent of the time by contracting their bodies. The researchers investigated something completely different, too. They made tests to see whether the learning would be retained if the planarian was cut in two. This procedure is not as drastic as it sounds, because the flatworm has the happy ability to regenerate its body when cut in two, ten, or even a hundred pieces. A tiny piece from the tail end will grow into an entirely new body, complete with brain.

Not too surprisingly, the head ends of the worms when re-generated and retrained showed that they had retained as much

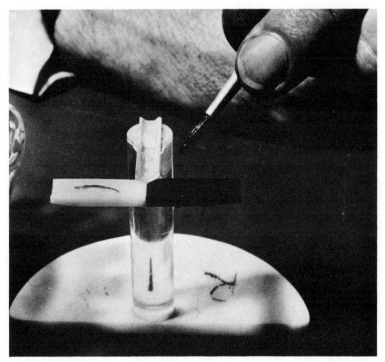

"Light conditioning" a flatworm to run a maze in a certain direction.

learning as a group of control planaria. What was amazing was the fact that the tail ends did just as well! Further tests showed that cutting a flatworm into several pieces resulted in several regenerated worms each with as much learning as the original. Published reports of these startling results were received with a jaundiced eye by many scientists, particularly when several labo-ratories reported failure to duplicate the learning experiments.

However, over the years more than twenty laboratories in many parts of the world eventually repeated the flatworm experiments successfully.

McConnell now had a planarian by the tail and for a while was not quite sure how to explain it. If the brain was in the head and memory resided there, how could the tail end of a flatworm regenerate a brain as learned as the original? The only possible answer seemed to be by a mighty extension of chemical memory storage, a theory advanced earlier by Semon, Halstead, and Hydén, among others. These men had suggested that memory resided not at the synapses but within individual neurons. Instead of having all its knowledge in its flat head, the planarian was a swimming encyclopedia with learning diffused throughout its entire body.

Now McConnell went even further. The flatworm lacks the immune reaction of higher creatures, a companion characteristic to its ability to regenerate. If the head from one flatworm could be grafted on to the tail of another, how about grafting "memory molecules" from a trained flatworm into one not trained? This was such a scientific approach as to sound most unscientific, and McConnell may have had some doubts about conducting this experiment. He did proceed, however.

At first the experimenters began to suspect that their far-out idea was too far out. The crude grafts failed—no learning transfer was achieved. Next were "several fumbling attempts at injecting exudates from one beast to another," but this, too, was unavailing. At this point McConnell had an idea for what he himself described as a "more startling type of tissue transfer." It happened that the species of flatworm most used in the learning experiments was a voracious cannibal. In 1960 McConnell and his colleagues began with *Dugesia dorotocephala* a series of experiments in "cannibalistic transfer" of training. One result was that McConnell received the nickname of "Dr. McCannibal." Another result was success.

The first step in the new experiments was to train flatworms by using the light-shock techinque. These trained animals were then cut into small pieces and fed to hungry, untrained planaria. A control group was fed pieces of untrained flatworms. All the

Dr. James McConnell at work in his laboratory.

planaria were then given the training, and it was at once evident, according to McConnell, that those fed the "educated" flatworms were significantly superior to those fed untrained worms. For the first time in scientific history, learning appeared to have been transferred chemically from one animal to another. The old dream of eating the chief to acquire his wisdom took a step forward.

The experiments were repeated and made more sophisticated by using the "blind" training technique in which the psychologists did not know which group they were training. The remarkable evidence of learning transfer persisted. To say that this caused a stir in the scientific fraternity is putting it mildly. Other laboratories attempted the experiment and reported failure—some of them in caustic tones. The controversy raged in the pages of the journal *Science* for some time, with learned discourse and scientific proofs advanced by both sides.

In answer to critics who suggested that only an "excitatory" hormone or something of the sort was being transferred to make the animals more ready learners, McConnell arranged more subtle tests that he claimed showed stimulus-specific transfer of learning.

He and his colleagues trained flatworms to choose the light or the dark arm of a T-maze until they performed correctly 90 percent of the time. The trained animals were then chopped up and fed to untrained ones. Some of these worms were taught to enter the same arm of the maze as the donors had been trained to enter; the others were taught to enter the opposite arm. The latter group did less well than the "same arm" trainees but better than flatworms who had been fed untrained donors. To test further the theory of transfer, scientists fed some animals "conflicting instructions" from two donors trained to run opposite arms of the maze. The result was "conflict behavior"—turning, circling, and refusing to run the maze.

Among other scientists attempting the transfer experiments were William Corning and E. Roy John. Remembering the work of D. Ewen Cameron and his aged forgetfuls, Corning and John allowed half of their trained and transversely bisected planaria to regenerate in plain pond water and half in a weak solution of RNAse, the chemical that Cameron had found adversely affected memory. Interestingly, Corning and John found that both head and tail ends regenerated in pond water retained their learning. The head ends regenerated in RNAse did, too. However, the tail ends regenerated in RNAse completely forgot the training and took as long to relearn as did naïve animals.

Heeding the Corning and John results, McConnell transferred only RNA extract from trained flatworms to naïve animals, in contrast to the gross technique of mincing the whole body of the planaria. This process was complicated by the fact that five hundred trained donors were required in order to produce enough RNA to inject only ten untrained subjects. In all, McConnell used more than four thousand flatworms in the RNA experiments. The results were similar to the cannibalistic approach; planaria injected with trained RNA apparently acquired the training of the donors. McConnell admitted that the mass training and RNA injection experiments were "crudely performed." However, he points out that significant statistical results were obtained and that the tests were valid.

Now it was suggested that even though something was apparently happening in the flatworm experiments, this animal was unique as a subject. Would transfer of learning take place in animals of higher "intellect"? By 1964 experimenters in four countries were conducting the experiments with rats and mice. David J. Albert at McGill University in Montreal; Stanislav Reinis in Pilsen, Czechoslovakia; Georges Ungar at Baylor University Medical School in Houston; and Fjerdinstad, Nissen, and Roigard-Petersen at the University of Copenhagen all demonstrated learning transfer with these more intelligent subjects. Among transfer experimenters was Frank Rosenblatt, the perceptron inventor.

As befits the man who had founded a journal called *The Worm Runner's Digest,* McConnell had some pointed comments on learning in such lowly "beasts" as the flatworm:

> I think, quite seriously, that over the years we have worked with rats so much that we have learned to think like rats, and that this is the trait that enables us to train rodents so well. We know considerably less about the "mental abilities" of invertebrates— no one that I know of is yet able to "think" like a worm—and it is quite likely that these so-called "lower" animals are much more capable of achieving enduring behavioral modification than anyone now dreams.

Tests with vertebrates continued, of course, and with excellent results. In the department of psychology at the University of California at Los Angeles, Dr. Jacobson and co-workers extended their transfer tests to rats. Next, hamsters were trained and RNA extract taken from their brains was injected into the bellies of rats; the rats then demonstrated that they had acquired learning from the hamsters.

Returning to planaria, the researchers did more complicated experiments on three groups of worms with twenty-five in each group. One group was untrained. The second group was given shock and light stimuli—but at random. The third group received conditioning training with shock and light. The extract from the three groups was then injected into other planaria. Those receiving the RNA from trained worms responded to light flashes more than five times as often as those receiving the RNA from untrained planaria.

So far it apparently had been demonstrated that planaria could learn from planaria extract and rats from rat extract. Genetic research indicates that there is a basic similarity in the DNA and RNA of all creatures—would learning-conditioned RNA from a hamster teach a rat? Surprisingly, it did—or seemed to. Jacobson and his colleagues injected rats with hamster potion and tested them over a series of twenty-five tries at the task the hamsters had learned. Eight rats received RNA from untrained hamsters; uninjected rats formed the control group. The results announced were amazing, to say the least.

With a possible score of 25, three of the uninjected rats scored one success, and one scored two. The remaining four did not succeed even once in twenty-five tries. The rats injected with learning serum, however, did much, much better. The lowest score was four, and the other rats scored five, seven, eight, nine, nine, ten, and eleven out of 25. This was a total of sixty-three successes to five for the control rats, a difference that would be hard to attribute merely to chance.

Interestingly, the RNA extract was injected not only into the brains of rats but in some cases into their bellies. Somehow the smartness potion seemed to find its way to the proper control cells in the brain and taught the correct response to the rats who had received no conventional training.

Dramatic as these results were, they were still not generally accepted by the scientific fraternity. Indeed, the great success of the tests worked against their being taken at face value. Some wondered how RNA from the liver of the test animals rather than extract taken from the brains might work. And how could the conditioned RNA preserve its composition and quantity, because it is nearly all broken down into its constituent bases, and these in turn are oxidized in the liver.

Dr. Melvin Calvin at the University of California at Berkeley reported that he could not repeat the results of McConnell, Jacobson, and fellow workers. Whereas the UCLA workers had used maze learning and light conditioning, the U.C. experimenters relied on electric shock, water deprivation, and cold water immersion. Perhaps such tactics drained the RNA extract of its efficacy, for it was claimed that the RNA rats did no better in subsequent tests than did the control animals.

Planaria, as might be expected of cannibals, ingest food in lumps without breaking down protein and RNA molecules into simpler ones, and one scientist wondered if RNA could move from bodies of other animals past the "blood-brain barrier." Radioactive labeling tests were conducted, and these seemed to fail to prove that any RNA extract reached the brain. Furthermore, RNA was injected directly into the vesicles of the brains of the recipient rats, and experimenters reported no significant learning effect.

To answer criticism that perhaps planaria weren't actually capable of true learning, researchers began to demonstrate that the worms were capable of more than mere "conditioned sensiti-

Rat performing complex learning task by pressing bar in cage at proper time.

zation." In 1959 E. N. Emhart and C. Sherrick had trained planaria to run a *two-unit* T-maze, a much more difficult learning task than one maze. C. D. Griffard later trained planaria to respond to light by turning left and to a vibration by turning right. Here were two antagonistic conditioned responses established in the same planarian, an indication of relatively "higher learning" than the more simple training given previously.

Rat experiments became more sophisticated, too, and in 1966 McConnell began attempts to train rats in very difficult tasks and then to transfer this learning. These "magazine transfer" tasks involved teaching a rat to push a lever and then to run to another part of the training box where a dipper of milk was presented for only twenty seconds. Some rats never learned this two-part task, and those that did learned it in two separate steps. It is thus a fairly complex learning feat. As the table shows, rats injected with trained RNA succeeded; the others did not.

NUMBER OF RESPONSES FROM NAÏVE RATS INJECTED WITH RNA
FROM TRAINED AND UNTRAINED DONORS

Day	Rat injected with RNA from Brains of Trained Donors					Rat injected with RNA from Brains of Untrained Donors				
	1	2	5	7	10	3	4	6	8	9
1	11	6	26	9	2	2	2	4	2	0
2	55	13	55	2	46	0	3	0	0	1
3	60*	60	60	5	60	3	3	2	1	4
4	60	34	60	3	60	1	1	0	1	6
5		60	60	5	60	1	4	2	2	4
6				28		1	4	0	0	0
7				60		14	4	2	0	0
8				50		0	4	2	0	0
9				60		0	1	8	0	2
10						0	3	6	1	4

* Criterion is 60 responses in less than 30 minutes.

One Mind to Another   Attempts had been made to improve memory with drugs such as magnesium pemoline. Were the learning transfer experimenters merely improving their subjects' ability to learn? Perhaps learning transfer experiments were not transferring memory but instead were enhancing the ability to learn. The idea of an actual transfer of learning was hard for many scientists to swallow, and much humor was extracted from the notion of cannibalizing the knowledge of a teacher. The following satire was printed in a letter to *Science*, 22 December 1967:

Persistence Transfer

The following is a brief account of some preliminary experiments we have made that appear to demonstrate the transfer of certain innate characteristics from one oscilloscope to another. More specifically, our object was to see whether a Tektronix 502 oscilloscope could be converted to a storage oscilloscope with indefinite persistence. While this could, of course, be achieved by altering the tube and modifying the electrical circuits by conventional techniques it nevertheless seemed worthwhile to test whether transfer of persistence could be effected by an extract made from a storage oscilloscope. Accordingly, a Tektronix Storage scope (R.M. 564) was allowed to run until there was no doubt about (i) the persistence of traces on the tube face; (ii) the effectiveness of the erasure mechanism; (iii) the stability of the image with respect to X- and Y-axes. The machine was then pounded with a Sears Roebuck ballpeen hammer (Cat. No. 28B4652) on a Fisher Lab bench (Cat. No. B148) covered by a $\frac{1}{2}$-inch stainless steel plate. The hammering was continued until all the electronic components and the tube were reduced to sufficiently small pieces to pass through a filter made of 007-mesh nylon stocking (seamless). In several experiments (2) the chassis was also ground up on a benchtop grinder (Sears No. 5634), but this procedure was not followed routinely, as it did not seem to affect the results materially and was both time-consuming and tedious. The storage oscilloscope fragments (S.O.F.) were next washed for 24 hours in CCl_4 in a cold room, dried at 70° C for 12 hours and stored in stoppered jars (Fisher Cat. No. 6139). For the actual experiment, S.O.F. was sprinkled over the chassis of a

Tektronix 502 oscilloscope. The persistence of the after-glow was used as an index for evaluating the effects of this procedure. The complete results are shown in Table 1. In 9 out of 33 experiments

TABLE 1   PERSISTENCE OF TRANSFER

Fragments	Increased	Decreased	No Change
S.O.F.	15 (P < .001)	6	9
Control Fragments	3	3	3

there was no change in the persistence, in 6 there was a decrease in persistence, but in 18 there was an increase which was highly significant (<.001, 1-test). Control experiments in which non-storage oscilloscopes were extracted showed no change. While the average increase in persistence was not large—3.2 msec—it nevertheless suggested that some change had been wrought in the recipient oscilloscope by the S.O.F. Another point of interest was that such affected oscilloscopes required far fewer alterations in their circuitry to convert them to storage oscilloscopes. The mechanism by which such changes are brought about is not clear as yet. Experiments are in progress to see how such information is transferred from machine to machine. In other experiments, standing patterns are being stored in the donor oscilloscope before preparing the S.O.F. with the expectation that similar patterns of persistence may occur in the recipient. The electronic uses of this procedure if further developed could be wide-spread.

J. G. Nicholls, D. A. Baylor
W. O. Wickelgren, J. Rosenthal
A. R. Martin, W. Betz
W. K. Chandler, H. Fein
A. E. Stuart, A. L. Finn
M. Odurih, R. A. Ridge

Department of Physiology,
Yale University School of Medicine
New Haven, Connecticut 06510

However, just at the height of the ridicule Baylor Medical School reported a new series of experiments that seemed to prove the transfer not just of general learning ability but also of specific learning. And the conclusion was that something other than RNA was doing the trick. In experiments conducted by Georges Ungar of Baylor Medical School, a different approach was taken. Because the work of McConnell, Jacobson, and others *might* indicate only a speeding up of learning, Ungar sought positive proof of the acquired knowledge of a *specific* ability.

Typhoid proteins entering the body for the first time produce antibodies that fight the invaders, as we have seen. The body cells that manufacture such antibodies thus "learn from experience." Years later a new invasion of typhoid is met with a vigorous release of antibodies. And it has been pointed out that the acquired drug tolerance of a mother can be transferred to the embryo in her womb. This is an acknowledged transfer of chemical learning. However, teaching the embryo a subject like arithmetic through the placenta is another, more difficult, trick.

It has been suggested that all that can be transferred is a "trigger" that activates a built-in memory circuit, that a complex memory resides not in one neuron or brain cell but in a system of cells. How an extract injected or taken internally can set a myriad of memory switches in just the right order is a mystery. The fact remains that in some experiments it *seemed* that the learning of one rat was imparted via a hypodermic needle to another rat. The fact that a large block of knowledge or a complex learning task was not involved does not disprove meaningful learning transfer. If even a tiny bit of learning can be transferred, the principle is proved. More sophisticated learning strings together these tiny bits—an analogy is the concept of dots on a TV screen being either white or black and thus building the image. The pioneer "Nipkow disk" was a crude forerunner, but it led to the modern color television receiver.

The immune reaction in the body can be classed as a form of learning, a similar phenomenon, that of drug tolerance, can also be thought of as learning because it results from experience. By injecting extracts from the brain of tolerant animals, Ungar had been able to induce drug tolerance in animals with no experience with that particular drug. Here is a technique that seems more closely allied with vaccine injections than with memory transfer. However, Ungar was encouraged enough by the drug tolerance transfer to attempt the transfer of more obviously learned behavior in rats.

The tolerance of sound is called habituation. An individual originally responsive to sound can be trained to tolerate it, as Ungar showed with rats. Originally, the rats were startled but through training the startle response was decreased to 10 percent or less. This 90 percent learning figure is the same criterion used by McConnell in his flatworm experiments. Ungar then injected brain extracts from trained rats into untrained rats and found that their startle responses were only about 50 percent, significantly less than normal for untrained animals. Next the Baylor workers succeeded in transferring light-dark discrimination and avoidance responses.

Ungar and his colleagues also trained rats that had a natural bias for turning in one direction in a Y-maze to turn in the other direction. This experiment differed from the Jacobson experiments in that each rat was taught to turn in the direction opposite to that which his genetic heritage told him to go. The rats achieved 90 percent accuracy in a period ranging from three to eighteen days.

An extract was then taken from the educated rats' brains by means of complicated dialysis techniques. In three different concentrations this extract was injected into three groups of mice. One group exhibited no natural turning tendency, one a tendency to turn right, and one a tendency to turn left. It was found that when a rat with a left tendency received extract from a right-trained rat, it was most likely to turn right; that is, against its natural tendency. Thus the experimenters claimed that the extract imparted two distinct instructions from the donors: first, to run in a certain direction and second, to run opposite to the normal tendency. When the extract bias was the same as the normal bias in the recipient rat, no transfer of learning took place, or there was even a reversal of instructions.

When injected with right-turn extract, mice with a left-turning bias increased their right turns from 31 percent to 49 percent, 57.5 percent, 56 percent, 57.5 percent, and 65 percent in five successive days. Right-biased rats with left-turn extract injections increased their left turns from 12 percent to 27 percent, 30 per-

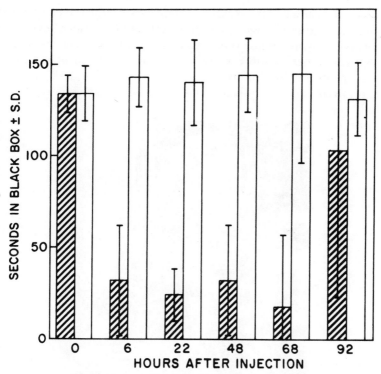

Injections of brain extract from rats trained to avoid dark induced similar behavior in untrained rats. Dark columns represent performance of rats injected with extract from trained rats; white columns represent control group injected with extract from untrained rats. Note that the rats injected with extract from rats trained to avoid the dark demonstrated similar avoidance for about three days and then began to revert to natural preference for dark.

cent, 27 percent, 42.5 percent, and 41 percent over a five-day period. Of 374 mice that received injections from trained rat brains, 272 behaved in accordance with the predictions of the Ungar-Irwin theory. Of 131 control mice that received injections from untrained rats, only 11 behaved as did the donor mice.

Dr. Ungar continued his experiments and transferred other bits of learning. One of these was a learned fear of the dark. Normally rats prefer a dark place to a light one. With electric shocks Ungar and his colleagues taught rats to fear the dark and to go instead to the light environment. In a long series of experiments involving hundreds of rats, Ungar established conclusively that rats injected with a preparation from the brain of trained rats spent only half the time learning to avoid the dark as did rats injected with extracts from the brains of untrained mice.

Dr. Georges Ungar, of Baylor University, and one of the rats used in learning-transfer experiments.

Ungar summarizes all the experiments made in his laboratory, which include the transfer of five "paradigms" or learning feats: habituation, conditioned avoidance, escape, light discrimination, and passive avoidance. Of 978 animals given extracts from trained donors, 697, or 71 percent, showed acquired learning. Of

329 control animals injected with material from untrained rats, only 59, or 18 percent, showed responses indicating learning. For the tests as a whole, Ungar calculates a probability of only one in a thousand that these results could have been due to chance.

Although the early Baylor experiments are subject to the criticism that only a general stimulating effect on learning was being transferred, or that stress rather than actual learning was being transferred, Ungar feels that the more stringent controls applied in later tests have ruled out such objections. Certainly his control techniques, including sophisticated "cross transfer," seem careful enough to eliminate chance results. Analysis of the brain extracts that Ungar used showed evidence that peptides (amino acid derivatives, from hydrolysis of proteins) rather than nucleic acid sequences were the learning factor. Here his results seem in disagreement with those of McConnell and others, because RNAse did not affect the transfer material but proteases did. Furthermore, Ungar found that there were specific transfer materials for each type of learning. For example, the sound habituation factor is destroyed by chymotrypsin; dark avoidance, by trypsin; and step-down avoidance, by both these substances. Ungar states that to produce behavioral effects by imparting specific information, each effect must be the result of a distinct molecular entity. He agrees with Hydén that a comparatively short amino acid sequence is ample to account for the coding of memory, and he reports that analysis indicates a chain length of eight to twelve amino acid residues (compared with Rosenblatt's theorized seven) for all three above learning factors.

Frank Rosenblatt also reported that peptides were the transfer factors isolated in his experiments. Ungar suggests that although the peptide is the active factor, it may be present in the RNA fractions that other workers claim to be the active material in transfer. He says further that RNA might act as the transfer factor in planaria and, when it is administered intracisternally, in mammals. In experiments where it is injected intraperitoneally, he feels that it is unlikely that the RNA would penetrate the blood-brain barrier. However, some peptides, including vasopressin, ACTH, MSH, and substance P, are known to penetrate this barrier and to reach the brain.

Interestingly, the transfer of specific learning factors has been duplicated in four of the six laboratories that sought to repeat Ungar's work. Late in 1968 Ungar told assembled scientists at the American Association for the Advancement of Science that his experiments showed an overwhelming probability that learned information can be transferred chemically under appropriate experimental conditions.

Compromise Solution With arguments similar to those of Rosenblatt in Chapter Ten, Ungar offers a solution to the impasse between the "connectionists," who favor electrical circuit pathways, and the molecular memory partisans. The molecular hypothesis, he says, is not only compatible with the complexities of differentiation in the nervous system but can also explain the memory trace pathways by a "mechanism of chemical recognition between neurons." The molecular memory approach, which permits linking of cells of the same category, is an extension and refinement of the genetic coding. This approach could permit differentiation of innate or genetic pathways and could also aid in creating new neural connections postulated for learning and memory.

For Ungar the beauty of this approach is a common explanation for innate *and* learned behavior. He points out that prior to any learning, animals respond to stimuli through inborn neural pathways. New, learned pathways are probably created, he says, by the simultaneous or near-simultaneous firing of neurons of different pathways. Increased permeability of synaptic structures may result in an interchange and a combination of "recognition molecules" of the two pathways and thus create new synaptic connections. (It is interesting that Ungar repeats almost exactly Pavlov's guess concerning the formation of new neural connections during classical conditioning.)

Ungar assumes that training synthesizes great amounts of chemical or molecular "connectors" and that this is the extract that binds itself to the proper sites in brains injected with extract. Here he makes an important observation. Because the brain probably manufactures the transfer factors only during the early period of intensive training, only this learning and not innate or long-established memory can ever be transferred. It is interesting to recall that Hydén's experiments showed that the RNA amount and content returned to their original values within about twenty-four hours after learning.

Tackling the short-term/long-term memory problem, Ungar suggests that the combination of molecular connectors creates only a temporary facilitation at the synapses. For the memory to become a lasting one, the affected neurons must synthesize, perhaps through the activation of previously repressed DNA sequences.

Ungar sums up his beliefs about the memory transfer mechanism as follows:

> According to the connector hypothesis, the molecular code of acquired information represents a system of road signs or signposts which directs the flow of impulses along the organized channels of the brain across the junctions created by learning. These coded molecules have meaning only in terms of the neural network, just as a road map can be used only in reference to an existing highway system.
>
> A "memory trace" or "engram" is probably represented in the brain by a neural circuit whose neurons are able to recognize each other because the synapses linking them are marked by the same connector molecule. The significant point that distinguishes the brain from an electronic computer is the chemical nature of the connection between the functional units. The computer is no doubt the best model that has yet been proposed for the nervous system provided one recognizes that the brain is not an electronic but a chemical computer.

Ungar has a further interesting comment on the importance of the transfer studies that seems to downgrade their immediate results:

> Chemical transfer represents a "playback" of the [memory] code. The phenomenon of transfer itself is of secondary importance and its possibilities are probably limited. The most significant point is that it can be used as a bioassay for the study and identification of the pathway-specific molecules and give us an insight into the code in which the brain handles information.

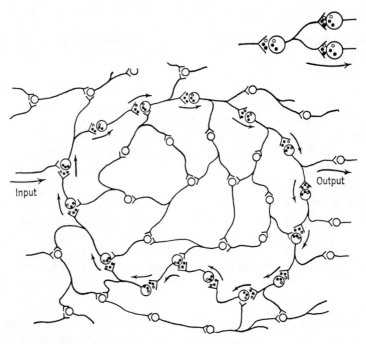

"Directional" molecular memory trace. Coded dots represent signposts for neuron circuit.

Thus Ungar neatly synthesizes the older connectionist view and the new molecular or chemical approach, a compromise that for some may be *too* neat, too tidy a melding of different theories of memory.

Instant Learning   McConnell seems unwilling to assign to chemical memory merely the position of "signpost" on a neural pathway:

> We defined learning as being "a relatively enduring behavioral change," sometimes adding the phrase "brought out through practice" to this definition. Yet, if learning has a biochemical basis, if the engram is really just an alteration in an RNA molecule inside some cell, then it should eventually be possible to

specify precisely which chemical changes are associated with which behavioral changes. Once the chemistry is known, we should be able to form engrams in a wide variety of ways. It is very likely that we could synthesize the necessary chemicals in a test tube and then inject the engram (knowledge) directly into the animal's cells just as we apparently can now "feed" engrams to cannibal flatworms. Once the "knowledge" became functional (inside the animal), the organism would show 'a relatively permanent behavioral change' without ever having directly experienced any contiguity whatsoever between stimuli and/or responses. From merely observing the animal's behavior after the engram became active, we could not, for the life of us, tell whether the animal had "learning in the regular fashion" or whether it had acquired the engram in a more direct manner. . . .

What a change it will make in our educational system if much of what man must learn during his too-short lifetime can be injected into him chemically!

What a change, indeed!

Chapter Thirteen

MEMORY AND THE FUTURE

Over the ages man's power of memory has greatly increased. In the foreseeable future memory is not going to increase greatly as a result of natural causes; such changes are now up to man. He has altered his environment and is now experimenting with transplants and artificial replacements for parts of his own body. And difficult though understanding may be, his mind nevertheless contains the seeds of inquiry that guarantee that he will pursue the search until he reaches that understanding. The results will be interesting, to say the least.

We use our memory to predict, just as a ballistic computer uses its mechanical or electrical-electronic memory to foretell accurately the site of a future target. The searchers for the engram have learned much that now resides in their memories and that will doubtless help them complete the task. And what will completion bring? It may be necessary to cross the line between accurate prediction and wishful prophecy even to suggest roughly the benefits that full knowledge of the anatomy of memory will bring to mankind.

At the very least, fewer people should be mentally defective in years to come. Already it is known that anoxia and certain other chemical deficiencies cause some of the unfortunate mental defects that Galton found at one end of his general distribution curve. The medical fraternity's working knowledge of the insides of the black box should guarantee that more of us will arrive in this world with a full genetic complement of neurons, properly prewired. With corrective techniques such as those Dr. Heyns suggested, everyone may be born with a better mental start.

A second fairly safe prediction is that knowledge of the memory mechanism will make it possible and perhaps a routine procedure to retrain more adequately those who have suffered brain damage. Already, with a groping knowledge of how we remember and learn and recall, specialists are able to give a great amount of aid to those suffering from accidental damage or from dysfunctions of various kinds.

We have seen that a better memory springs generally from better methods of learning. Although educators, with an assist from psychologists and their black-box approach, have already done an estimable job in the teaching of learning, a definite knowledge of what goes on in the memory circuits should be useful in the development of learning techniques. When searchers at last track down the ultimate particles of short-term and long-term memory (if they prove to be separate entities), their maps and blueprints will be of great value to those who deal with the biocomputer of the brain. Thus far teachers have approximated a race-car mechanic who knows nothing of what is under the hood but nevertheless works to achieve more speed and better handling through purely inferential methods.

Tachistoscopy may come into its own and speed reading become a reality, with thousands of words a minute assimilated comprehensively at the unconscious level, yet firmly fixed in the memory for later conscious recall. Combinations of sensory stimuli may yield faster and more comprehensive learning in addition to better retention and recall. Sight, sound, and motor learning may be combined into a form of super learning. Other channels may exist for transmitting information to the brain's memory banks; electrical stimuli applied with the right amplitude and frequency modulation and in the proper location may supplant conventional teaching, which involves the perception of the real thing.

If milk produces mighty memories, there may be other potions that will do even better. Beyond all the "Cylert smoke" there may be a fire of truth that will someday be used to light a torch of better understanding. The aged may be treated with drugs, including RNA or other nucleic material, to arrest the death of brain cells that cause memory loss. Decades ago science fiction told of mind doctors who with a tiny needle excise "bad engrams" and thus heal mental patients. Such a potent exciser of sickness might supplant present psychiatric practitioners.

Although such suggestions raise some hackles, it is conceivable that learning may be imparted chemically, *à la* Gulliver's "Cephalick tincture." Learning transfer of this nature is as unpalatable an idea to some as it apparently was to the schoolboys in Swift's parable, but the idea is hardly more different from conventional learning than space travel is from horse-and-buggy days.

There is the clear and present danger that memory knowledge can be subverted; Huxley, Orwell, and others have written cautionary tales spelling out the strategy and the tactics for such mind control. But as with nuclear energy, aircraft, and space travel, we must accept that danger and guard against its offsetting the potential good to be realized by improving our knowledge of memory.

The memory revolution, then, may herald a millennium or produce an age of brainwashing tyranny. There is, of course, a third possibility. Those who say man's mind cannot comprehend itself may be correct—in which case memory will remain the black box it has historically been. Win, lose, or draw, the search for the engram goes on.

INDEX

Zegarnik

Illustration Credits

Credits are listed by page numbers.